Christine de Pizan was born in Venice and raised in Paris at the court of Charles V of France. Widowed at the age of twenty-five, she turned to writing as a source of comfort and income, and went on to produce a remarkable series of books, on subjects including poetry, politics, chivalry, warfare, religion and philosophy. She is considered to be France's first female professional writer.

This is the first translation into modern English of Christine de Pizan's major political work, *The Book of the Body Politic*. Written during the Hundred Years War, it discusses the education and behavior appropriate for princes, nobility and common people, so that all classes can understand their responsibilities towards society as a whole. A product of a time of civil unrest, *The Book of the Body Politic* offers a medieval political theory of interdependence and social responsibility from the perspective of an educated woman.

CAMBRIDGE TEXTS IN THE
HISTORY OF POLITICAL THOUGHT

CHRISTINE DE PIZAN
*The Book of the Body Politic*

# CAMBRIDGE TEXTS IN THE HISTORY OF POLITICAL THOUGHT

*Series editors*

RAYMOND GEUSS
*Reader in Philosophy, University of Cambridge*

QUENTIN SKINNER
*Regius Professor of Modern History in the University of Cambridge*

Cambridge Texts in the History of Political Thought is now firmly established as the major student textbook series in political theory. It aims to make available to students all the most important texts in the history of western political thought, from ancient Greece to the early twentieth century. All the familiar classic texts will be included, but the series does at the same time seek to enlarge the conventional canon by incorporating an extensive range of less well-known works, many of them never before available in a modern English edition. Wherever possible, texts are published in complete and unabridged form, and translations are specially commissioned for the series. Each volume contains a critical introduction together with chronologies, biographical sketches, a guide to further reading and any necessary glossaries and textual apparatus. When completed, the series will aim to offer an outline of the entire evolution of western political thought.

*For a list of titles published in the series, please see end of book.*

# CHRISTINE DE PIZAN

# The Book of the Body Politic

EDITED AND TRANSLATED BY

## KATE LANGDON FORHAN

*Associate Professor of Political Science*
*Siena College*

CAMBRIDGE
UNIVERSITY PRESS

CAMBRIDGE UNIVERSITY PRESS
Cambridge, New York, Melbourne, Madrid, Cape Town, Singapore,
São Paulo, Delhi, Dubai, Tokyo, Mexico City

Cambridge University Press
The Edinburgh Building, Cambridge CB2 8RU, UK

Published in the United States of America by Cambridge University Press, New York

www.cambridge.org
Information on this title: www.cambridge.org/9780521422598

First published 1994
Fifth printing 2007

*A catalogue record for this publication is available from the British Library*

*Library of Congress Cataloguing in Publication data*
Christine, de Pisan, ca. 1364–ca. 1431.
[Livre du corps de policie, English]
The book of the body politic / Christine de Pizan: edited and translated by
Kate Langdon Forhan.
p.   cm. – (Cambridge texts in the history of political thought)
Includes bibliographical references (p. ) and index.
ISBN 0 521 41050 9 (hardback) – ISBN 0 521 42259 0 (paperback)
1. Education of princes.   2. Monarchy.   3. English language – Middle English,
1100–1500 – Texts.   I. Forhan, Kate Langdon, 1949–
II. Title.      III. Series.
JC393.A3P513 1994
321'.6 – dc20    93–37130 CIP

ISBN 978-0-521-41050-2 Hardback
ISBN 978-0-521-42259-8 Paperback

To
My Students at Siena College
and
Jean Blancard Forhan

# Contents

# Acknowledgments

I should like to thank Siena College, the Arts Division, and the Department of Political Science for material and personal support for this volume. In particular, I should like to credit the members of the Siena College Medieval Group (Professors Pam Clements, Celia Diamond, Margaret Hannay, Mary Meany, and Cary Nederman), Sean Maloney of the Siena College Library, and Ms Ellen Johnson from the Faculty Support Office. I should also like to acknowledge the assistance of the Bibliothèque Nationale, Paris, and to thank its helpful and knowledgeable staff. I am also grateful to an anonymous reader and to Professor Quentin Skinner, both acting for Cambridge University Press for their insightful comments. To Professor Cary Nederman, erstwhile colleague, generous and constant friend, my gratitude as always.

By far my greatest debt rests with my students at Siena, past and present, and my own teachers, the late George Armstrong Kelly, Richard Flathman, Marvin Zetterbaum, and especially my mother, Jean Blancard Forhan. It is to them that this volume is dedicated. Without their inspiration on the one hand and guidance on the other, no scholarly accomplishments would mean very much.

# Introduction

Considered to be the first woman of letters of France, Christine de Pizan (*c.*1364–*c.*1430) was born in Venice. She was the daughter of Thomas de Pizan, medical doctor and astrologer, whose training at the prestigious University of Bologna brought him an appointment to the court of Charles V of France. In 1369 he settled his young family in Paris which became their permanent home. Christine was encouraged in her education both by her father and her young husband, Etienne du Castel, whom she married in 1380. Christine's love of learning and familiarity with court life brought their reward when she was suddenly left a young widow at the age of twenty-five, with three young children, a widowed mother, and an orphaned niece to support. Christine turned to a life of letters at first for consolation and later for income, writing a series of remarkable books that included works of poetry, biography, politics, chivalry, warfare, religion and philosophy for a variety of wealthy and noble patrons.

When *The Book of the Body Politic* was written between late 1404 and 1407, France was hovering on the brink of civil war. The intricate and complicated struggle between the French and the English commonly called the Hundred Years War (1337–1453) was an extension of the conflict between these two developing nations that had begun in the twelfth century. Complicated by family rivalries and changing ideas about property, inheritance, sovereignty, and the feudal relationship, France had "won" the first round, ending with the Treaty of Paris in 1259, although England had retained its possession of Aquitaine, held as a fief from the French kings. As the French economy strengthened, English economic and political interests in Aquitaine were threatened. In 1337, Edward III of England announced that he was claiming the French throne, on the grounds of superior hereditary right. Since he was a grandson of Philip IV through his mother, and the present king, Philip VI, was only a nephew, Edward claimed to be in the direct line of succession.

Philip responded by confiscating Aquitaine as punishment for this rebellion against an overlord. This second phase of the war was a disaster for France. The French nobility was decimated at the battles of Crecy (1346) and Poitiers (1356), and ultimately humiliated when King John of France (1350–1364) was captured and carried off to England. The ensuing crisis and confusion included a peasant revolt against high taxes and the losses of war, marauding bands of soldiers terrorizing the people, greedy nobles trying to extend their privileges, as well as attempts by the Estates General to control abuses and reform taxes – all of which threatened the authority of the regent, John's son Charles. John finally negotiated his release in 1360 in exchange for Aquitaine and three million gold ecus, but complications returned him to English hands and he died in 1364 with the final steps of the treaty not taken.

The intelligent and responsible rule of Charles V (r.1364–1380) allowed a brief recovery, but was followed by confusion and struggle for power when he died in September 1380, leaving his heir, Charles VI (r.1380–1422) not quite twelve years old. The king had named his own brother, Louis, duke of Anjou, (d.1384) to be regent for the young king with two of the boy's other relatives, the dukes of Burgundy and Bourbon, to be his guardians. Duke John of Berry, with no official role as regent or guardian, nonetheless controlled about a third of France through his own estates. Although the young prince managed to escape the legal control of his uncles once he became an adult, he could not elude their machinations and ambitions, and was very much under the influence of his younger and more able brother, Louis of Orleans. The chaos was compounded when, in 1392, the twenty-four-year-old king suffered his first attack of insanity, which afflicted him periodically for the rest of his life. The growing disability of Charles VI trapped France between the two powerful personalities of the king's younger brother, Louis, duke of Orleans and his uncle, Philip "the Bold," duke of Burgundy, and after Philip's death in 1404, that of his son, John, "the Fearless." The gap between the royal houses widened until on November 23, 1407, Louis of Orleans was murdered by an assassin, Raoul d'Anquentonville, who had been hired by John the Fearless. The duke fled for his safety, but in an attempt to obtain pardon from the king, a defence of his actions was written and proclaimed at court by Master Jean Petit of the University of Paris, justifying the assassination of Louis on the grounds of tyrannicide. Jean Petit's argument, that tyrannicide is not only justified but meritorious, was taken from John of Salisbury's *Policraticus*. The widowed duchess of Orleans found support and protection for her young son, Charles of Orleans, in Bernard, count of Armagnac, who was now the leader of the opposition to Duke John of Burgundy.

Things were not much better in England. The murder of Richard II in 1400, the adventurous spirit of Henry IV and his need for additional revenue, clashed with French attempts at aggrandizement and protection of commercial interests. The papal schism from 1378 to 1417 left Europe without an acceptable mediator, and in fact each of the papal rivals encouraged the nation supporting him – Urban VI the English and Clement VII the French.

In France, the quarrels, ambitions, greed, and self-interest exhibited by the members of the royal family over the next thirty years brought the nation to civil war and impoverished it with heavy taxation. The political bankruptcy of the nobility was further demonstrated when the Burgundians and the Armagnacs each made overtures to the English, hoping to have their help to destroy the other. The English king, Henry V (r.1413–1422) had his own agenda – to seize the throne of France – and invaded in 1415, crushing the French army at Agincourt. Rather than rallying to defend the kingdom, the Burgundians continued to fight the Armagnacs, openly allying themselves with the English in 1420. The alliance allowed the English to impose the Treaty of Troyes on Charles VI, which made Henry V Regent of France whenever the king was incapacitated by his mental illness, as well as making Henry heir to the throne. This effectively disinherited the Dauphin, Charles of Guyenne, third and only living son of Charles VI. But both Henry V and Charles VI died in 1422, leaving Henry's infant son, Henry VI, nominally king of France and England.

In the meantime, the son of Charles VI had been a virtual prisoner of the Armagnacs in the south of France, without a hope of rule. But the inspiration of a young girl, Joan of Arc, rallied the dispirited French to win the battle of Orleans in 1429, the first French victory for many years. Soon afterwards, the Dauphin was crowned Charles VII and the French were encouraged to retake their cities. Joan's capture by the Burgundians, and her subsequent trial and execution for heresy at the hands of the English in 1431, further inspired the French to continue until final victory in 1453.

Christine de Pizan was far more than a spectator of these events. Several of her works were directly inspired by them and were intended to ameliorate or rectify the situation of the French people by recalling their rulers to what she believed were their proper duties. For example, the misfortunes of the French as well as personal experience inspired her work entitled *The Mutability of Fortune*, presented to the duke of Burgundy on January 4, 1404. The contrast of the present with the wise rule of the former king is apparent in her biography of Charles V, *The Book of the Deeds and Good Customs of King Charles V*, which was commissioned by the duke of Burgundy in 1404. *The Book of Deeds of Arms and Chivalry* was a handbook on warfare and military ethics written for the Dauphin, Louis of Guyenne, a few years later. In 1410, she wrote *Lamentation on the Troubles of France*, in the form of a letter to John, duke of Berry. This letter, which may have been written at the request of John the Fearless, Berry's nephew and duke of Burgundy after the death of his father Philip in 1404, addresses all the princes of France, describing vividly the devastation of civil war and the horrors to come if there is no peace. In 1412, she began *The Book of Peace*, which was also dedicated to the Dauphin. It was finished in 1413, its theme horribly relevant, and a copy was presented to the duke of Berry in January 1414.

After the battle of Agincourt, Christine wrote *The Letter Concerning the Prison of Human Life*, dedicated to Marie of Berry, duchess of Bourbon, whose husband was a prisoner of war in England. The work was written to console the women of France mourning the dead and prisoners of Agincourt. Her last known work is *The Story of Joan of Arc* written at the time of Joan's greatest glory before her trial and execution.

This was the context within which the *The Book of the Body Politic* made its appearance between 1404 and 1407, shortly before the assassination of Louis of Orleans. Although it was dedicated to Charles VI and the princes of the royal family, Christine mentions in *The Book of Peace* that *The Book of the Body Politic* was written for the particular benefit of the Dauphin, Louis of Guyenne. The political situation was so violent and explosive that aspects of the work, especially the *exempla*, which might otherwise seem conservative or even commonplace, are revealed as quite shrewd and daring. They include accounts of a prince deposed from office for disrespect to the church, of several rulers whose devotion to the law demanded the execution or punishment of their own sons, of princes who are rewarded for their commitment to the public good to their personal cost, as well as warnings about the dangers faced by tyrants, i.e., "the higher the tower, the greater the risk from a small stone." Christine uses a conventional genre to deliver a warning to princes about the consequences of misrule. In a time of civil war, her position was delicate and her advice discreet, but there is, nonetheless, a warning to tyrants.

The works for which Christine is best known today were written to defend and instruct women: *The Book of the City of Ladies* and *The Book of the Three Virtues* (also called *The Treasury of the City of Ladies*). *The Book of the Body Politic*, however, was written for a young man, the fourteen-year-old heir to the throne, Louis of Guyenne. This political treatise is an example of a "mirror for princes." Its purpose was to instruct as well as entertain the prince, with the goal of transforming him into a model king.

The "mirror for princes," or prince's handbook, was an important genre for the development of political thought throughout the Middle Ages. It served as a transmitter of many classical Greek and Roman ideas about politics, but also altered them, giving them Christian rhetorical and political significance. As a genre, the mirror for princes follows certain conventions. It typically begins with a "humility topos." The author disclaims any particular linguistic or political ability to advise the prince, but accepts the responsibility either because his work was commissioned by him, or because the author believes it to be in the best interests of the kingdom. The substantive discussion of political ideas is organized around a narrative order – the transformation of the prince into an ideal king. In some works this is presented in part as a physical transformation, and the advice includes principles of nutrition, hygiene, and instruction in a variety of subjects. In others the transformation is metaphorical; the prince's moral and intellectual infancy is gradually exchanged for a mature wisdom and virtue. The text is characteristically enlivened by *exempla* from Scriptural and classical stories of good and bad rulers. All political mirrors emphasize the development of character, good judgment, and the classical virtues of courage, justice, temperance, and prudence, as well as the princely qualities of liberality, magnificence, generosity, and authority. The differences in mirrors stem from their authors' disagreements about the essential nature of kingship and the problems of ruling as well as the differences brought about by political culture and context.

*Exempla* provide a fascinating window onto medieval political ideas. To modern readers, *exempla* seem to be tedious stories interspersed between the "real" political ideas. But this is to misunderstand important aspects of medieval political culture. These books were meant to entertain and were often read aloud to an audience that wanted to hear a good adventure story with an emphatic moral. *Exempla* fulfilled that need, providing heroic stories from Roman or Greek history of admirable military and political leaders – or their evil counterparts. But *exempla* also provided a vehicle for political ideas and thus illuminate medieval political thought in a number of interesting ways. First, the "moral" of the story may be different from the one we would draw today. Some of Christine's stories of trickery in part II would seem to us unethical, yet Christine's audience might not have found them inconsistent with honor. Secondly, details of the story may have been changed from the classical source, so as to make the moral the medieval writer intends more pointed and explicit, or even radically different. For example, Christine's retelling in part I of the fable of the revolt of the limbs against the belly is a case in point. Originally found in Livy, this story was retold by many authors, such as Marie de France and John of Salisbury, but each draws a different political lesson. Thirdly, the writer's attempt to make the story intelligible to a particular audience may educate us about medieval customs or beliefs. Christine de Pizan's explanation of the Roman custom of the triumph, or the role of the consul in Roman political life, tells us not only about contrasting French practices, but also underline her themes, that noble behavior should be rewarded, or that military leaders should be responsible to others. Fourthly, *exempla* provide an application of abstract political principles, illustrating concepts such as justice or good rule. Stories of good and bad rulers are parables in a sense, making theoretical lessons concrete. Christine's stories of rulers who put the public good before their own, or who insist on the maintenance of justice even at personal cost, are very revealing about what she saw as the problems of her age.

For the medieval reader, *exempla* also provided a link with the Golden Age of the past, and a sense of historical continuity in a world that sometimes seemed in the process of disintegration. The Romans and Greeks were great warriors, wise in government and law, and yet they too experienced defeat, capture, suffering, betrayal, injustice, and death as did their counterparts in the Middle Ages. These stories brought a sense of being part of a great tradition. As a consequence, many medieval writers felt a real sense of kinship with Aristotle, Seneca, or Cicero, and accorded them great reverence. Like other writers, Christine de Pizan showed this by referring to Aristotle by the title "the Philosopher" rather than by name.

Finally, *exempla* were authoritative. Authoritative writing was the primary kind of evidence considered as proof of an argument. In Christine's case, if she – an insignificant woman – says that "justice is rendering to each his due," this assertion may carry little weight, but if she quotes from Aristotle, she has proved her point. Certain writers were considered to be particularly authoritative in politics. In *Body Politic*, Christine de Pizan cites (pseudo-)Plutarch and Aristotle. In *Book of Wisdom*, she cites extensively a work attributed to Seneca, *Formula for an Honest Life* (in fact the work of Martin of Braga). All three were known as philosophers who had instructed princes, in these cases Trajan, Alexander the Great, and Nero respectively. The Roman Emperor Trajan in particular, whose story Christine tells in *The Book of Peace*, was considered throughout the Middle Ages as the ideal king, so good that St. Gregory prayed for his soul and Dante placed him in Paradise even though Trajan was a pagan. Cicero and Boethius were also significant sources in the tradition because of their authority as philosopher-statesmen who suffered as a consequence of their politics. The choice of these particular authorities gave additional weight to the writer's message.

For the medieval reader or listener, *exempla* were not merely illustrative but were the whole point of the book, the pearls of wisdom strung together by the author's prose. Today, we ought to take them very seriously, asking ourselves about the story's moral and what its protagonist is intended to illustrate, or what kind of behavior he or she models. This entails a kind of reading between the lines that is both unfamiliar and difficult since we lack the shared non-written culture to which medieval writers often allude. We can get a glimpse of that shared culture if we are familiar enough with the literature of the period to pick up references to Scripture, mystery plays, songs, liturgy and saints' lives that were part of common parlance.

*The Book of the Body Politic* makes use of all the traditions of the mirror genre to adapt the authoritative ideas of antiquity to the needs of practical politics. It addresses a central problem for those involved in an active life in the world in any age – how to conjoin a life of practical politics with the desire for the Good, for the love of wisdom. It is this use of the tradition itself that marks the work most profoundly.

*The Book of the Body Politic* takes its name and organizing theme from John of Salisbury's twelfth-century work, *Policraticus*, in which the political community is described as a body, with king as head, soldiers and administrative officers as the hands, and the peasants as the feet. While John of Salisbury attributes the metaphor to a letter from Plutarch to his pupil Trajan, most contemporary scholars see this as a polite fiction, and think this use of the image to be John's own. The human body had been used by other authors since the twelfth century to express interdependence and hierarchy, depending on the author's political views. But the *Policraticus* is more than just the source of an interesting political metaphor. It is a compendium of moral and political philosophy, and includes discussions on a variety of diverse but interrelated themes: on the vices peculiar to court life and their corresponding virtues, on the idea of justice and the nature of good government, on tyranny and the possible legitimacy of tyrannicide, and on the responsibility of kings and courtiers to become lovers of wisdom. By the late fourteenth century, the work was widely known and revered. Charles V, a noted bibliophile, had commissioned for his own library not only a new copy of the *Policraticus*, but a French translation as well. By the early fifteenth century, the selections on tyranny and tyrannicide assumed a new importance in the defense of the assassins of Louis of Orleans.

In Christine's work the metaphor is used primarily as an organizing theme, and is attributed directly to Plutarch without reference to John of Salisbury. This of course fulfills the need for an authoritative classical source for her work. The text suggests, however, that she knew the *Policraticus* well, especially John of Salisbury's discussions of flattery, astrology, and tyranny.

*The Book of the Body Politic* is arranged in three parts, corresponding to the major classes or "estates" of French society. Part I considers the education of the prince in detail – what he should eat, how he should dress, as well as the books, experiences, and ideas to which he should be exposed. Much of this discussion relies heavily on Giles of Rome's mirror for princes, *De regimine principum.*

This is followed by advice on how to govern: the choice of advisors and administrators, how to prevent corruption and bribery, the king's role with respect to the church, the importance of education and rhetorical skill. Here Christine's primary sources include John of Salisbury, Giles of Rome, and Brunetto Latini, and she refers to Aristotle's *Ethics* and *Politics* as well as his *Rhetoric* and *Metaphysics.* Her other major classical sources are Cicero (*On Duties* and *On Old Age*), Boethius' *Consolation of Philosophy*, with passing references to Seneca, Livy, Ovid, and Plato, and, among Christian authors, to Augustine, Anselm, and Ambrose. While the quotations are not always word-for-word, even if phrased as though they were, the references she cites tend to be accurate. However, they probably come from "florilegia," collections of excerpts from classical authors that were favourite source books for many medieval writers. The *exempla* in this part of the work come predominantly from Valerius Maximus' *Facta et Dicta Memorabilia* (*Memorable Words and Deeds*). His work is a huge collection of stories and anecdotes arranged according to subject-matter in a kind of encyclopedia of material for public speakers. To modern tastes, it is pompous and artificial, but it enjoyed tremendous popularity in the Middle Ages as a source of *exempla.* Christine herself felt obliged to explain why she quoted from him so often in part I, chapter 13, entitled 'Why Valerius is cited so much in this work.'

> For, as that same Valerius says, examples of virtue move one to desire honor and courage and to love of virtue more than simple words do, as Aristotle attests in the tenth book of the *Ethics.*

Therefore, in following the style of the noble author Valerius . . .
I am moved to show diverse examples of things that happened
to many magnificent men in the past, who are memorialized in
this book for their merit.

Part I also reflects Christine's reading in the choice of virtues she
believes important in the prince: piety, humility, kindness, mercy,
and chastity reflect the Christian tradition, liberality, justice, and love
of glory reveal the classical one. Her emphasis on learning and eloquence and her concern to differentiate the intelligent use of astrological principles from charlatanism and fatalism demonstrate her
humanist values.

Part II treats knights and nobles, and considers the nature and
behavior to be expected of this class. Although not explicitly stated
as such, her subject is the nature and meaning of nobility, which she
portrays as a quality of soul rather than of rank. She draws very
heavily on the Aristotelian notion of *hexis*, in Latin *habitus*, often
translated as "habit" or "disposition." Christine's term for this concept is "moeurs," which can be understood as habit, morals, manners, or even custom, depending on the context. For Christine, this
concept has important theoretical implications because it combines
public and private behavior, the world of morality with the world of
law. If the correct habits of virtue are inculcated early, they will be
reflected in the individual person's morals as well as in his or her
manners. In a world where political institutions had been enfeebled
by civil conflict and neglect, this reflects Christine's belief that personal responsibility is the cornerstone of political life. Part II cites
Valerius extensively for *exempla*, but also draws upon the *Epitome of
Military Topics* of Renatus Flavius Vegetius on Roman military customs and strategy.

Part III examines the common people: merchants, clergy, students,
and artisans as well as peasants. To the modern reader this may
appear unexceptional, but by comparison with John of Salisbury's
political "physiology," it must have seemed shocking. In his work,
the clergy are the soul of the body politic, without which the body is
dead. The position of the clergy among the lower "limbs" by Christine reveals her view that the clergy's role is a functional one. They
provide masses and prayers in the way that a baker provides bread –
important to society but not essential. Her society, both real and
ideal, has become much more secularized. Secondly, Christine's

"physiology" reveals changes in the political and economic structure of the medieval community. No longer is the traditional tripartite division into "those who pray, those who fight and those who work" sufficient to understand society. Merchants, students, and artisans do not fit easily into the three orders but are beginning to be recognized as having a separate political and economic role in society. Burghers are citizens who enjoy special privileges in their own right in their cities. Their leadership function is stressed by Christine when she describes them as protectors, advocates, and intercessors for the poorer members of their class.

While this is the shortest part of the book, it shows us a rare discussion of the responsibilities of common people – of whom Christine was one. It also shows most revealingly how much society had changed since the twelfth century use of the metaphor of the body politic. John of Salisbury can still hope that the institutional changes brought about by the codification of laws and legal institutions in the twelfth century will be sufficient in large part to guarantee good government. Christine has no such hope. Institutions have not been able to restrain the greed and pettiness of rulers and aristocrats, but perhaps the responsible burgher can. Hers is both the optimism and the pessimism of a newly educated and affluent class.

Part III also relies on material from Aristotle, Giles of Rome and John of Salisbury, but Christine often cites the Bible in part III as a guide to life for the common people. Here she explicitly uses quotations from the Pauline Epistles stressing obedience to civil authority, while at the same time, through her choice of *exempla*, making oblique references to political violence as a potential consequence of tyranny.

Christine de Pizan has been lavishly praised as the first female professional writer in France. Certainly she is of interest to historians for her detailed accounts of aspects of everyday life that are otherwise unavailable or only available through the eyes of male observers. Her mirrors for princesses illustrate the often invisible lives of women and children of every class. But as a political writer her significance has not been evaluated. She is sometimes dismissed as a mere compiler or as a conservative apologist for the ruling classes. Some might argue that she is not sufficiently philosophical, not distant enough from the immediate circumstances of early fifteenth-century France to be of lasting significance. Others might argue that she was not involved enough, not willing to seriously challenge the assumptions of her age. In fact, she has been described best by Charity Cannon Willard, her distinguished biographer and editor, in her introduction to *Le Livre de la Paix*:

> The noble and generous spirit of the woman shines through the prolixity, the clumsy and profuse style. Although lacking in qualities of real genius, she unstintingly used the talents that she had in behalf of her country. (p. 54)

Like Boethius or Cicero or John of Salisbury, who inspired her, her work and ideas are not without flaws, but the flaws stem from the attempt to conjoin a life of practical politics with the desire for the Good, for the love of wisdom.

This appreciation for the inseparability of politics and philosophy, of life in the world from the life of the mind, is best expressed by Christine de Pizan herself. As she addresses Dame Philosophy, in *L'Avision Christine*, she says, "tu es politique, car tu aprens a bien vivre."

# Note on the text

Christine's style in *Corps de Policie* is quite different from that of several of her other works. It is an example of the *style clergial*, a more formal kind of writing considered appropriate for her princely audience. To modern tastes, it is convoluted, redundant, and less lively than, for example, *City of Ladies.* Rather than attempting to render her style, my aim has been a lively rendition of her thought, and a sense of her appreciation of her sources, particularly her delight in *exempla.*

I have used the text edited by Robert Lucas, Christine de Pizan, *Livre de corps de policie* (Geneva, 1967), which is based on Bibliothèque Nationale f. fr. 12439, fols. 46v–225v. When a variant appears in other manuscripts that appears to make more sense in the context, I use the variant.

As an additional aid to the reader, a glossary has been included to provide brief biographical details (where available) of persons mentioned in the text as well as to elucidate concepts that may not be familiar to the reader. These words and names are marked with an asterisk (*) when they first appear in the text.

# Principal events in Christine de Pizan's life

c.1364    Birth of Christine de Pizan in Venice
c.1367    Thomas de Pizan, her father, accepts a position at the
          court of Charles V of France
1368      Birth of the Dauphin Charles, eldest son of Charles V
1371      Birth of Charles V's second son Louis, duke of Orleans
1377      Death of King Edward III of England; Richard II reigns
1378      Beginning of the papal schism
1380      Christine marries Master Etienne du Castel, court sec-
          retary and notary
          September 16, death of Charles V, the Dauphin becomes
          Charles VI
1381      Peasant Revolt (England)
c.1387    Death of Thomas de Pizan
1390      Death of Etienne du Castel
1392      Charles VI has first attack of mental illness
1394      Christine begins to write poetry
1396      Marriage of Richard II of England and Isabelle, daughter
          of Charles VI, brings treaty with England
1397      Christine's daughter, Marie, enters the royal Dominican
          convent of Poissy
1398      Christine's son, John, enters the service of the earl of
          Salisbury
1399      Murder of Richard II, Henry IV becomes king of
          England
          Beginning of Christine's public literary career

|      | |
|------|-|
|      | *The Letter of Othéa the Goddess to Hector (l'Epistre d'Othéa la Déesse a Hector)* |
| 1399 | *Cupid's Letter (l'Epistre au Dieu d'Amour)* |
| 1400 | *The Tale of Poissy (Le Dit de Poissy)* |
| 1402 | *The Tale of the Rose (Le Dit de la Rose)* |
| 1403 | *The Long Road of Learning (Le Livre de Longue Estude)* |
|      | *The Tale of the Shepherdess (Le Dit de la Pastoure)* |
| 1404 | Death of Philip "the Bold," duke of Burgundy, his son, John "the Fearless," inherits |
|      | *The Book on the Mutability of Fortune (Le Livre de Mutation de Fortune)* |
|      | *The Book of the Deeds and Good Customs of King Charles V (Le Livre des Fais et Bonnes Meurs du Roy Charles V)* |
| 1405 | *Christine's Vision (L'Avision Christine)* |
|      | *The Book of Deeds of Arms and of Chivalry (Le Livre de Fais d'Armes et de Chevalrie)* |
|      | *The Book of the City of Ladies (Le Livre de la Cité des Dames)* |
| 1406 | *Book of the Three Virtues: the Treasury of the City of Ladies (Le Livre des Trois Vertus: Le Trésor De la Cité des Dames)* |
|      | *The Book of the Body Politic (Le Livre de Corps de Policie)* |
| 1410 | *Lamentation on the Troubles of France (Lamentation sur les Maux de la France)* |
| 1413 | Popular uprising, the Cabochian Revolt in Paris |
|      | Henry IV dies, Henry V becomes king of England |
|      | *The Book of Peace (Le Livre de la Paix)* |
| 1415 | October 25, Battle of Agincourt |
| 1415 | Death of the Dauphin, Louis de Guyenne; John, duke of Touraine becomes Dauphin |
| 1416 | Death of the duke of Berry |
| 1417 | Death of Louis of Anjou and John of Touraine; Charles becomes Dauphin |
|      | End of the Great Schism |
|      | *Letter Concerning the Prison of Human Life (l'Epistre de la Prison de Vie Humaine)* |
| 1418 | In May, the people of Paris revolt, Bernard of Armagnac is murdered. Burgundian forces retake Paris. |
|      | Massacres force Christine and other prominent Parisians to flee. Christine apparently enters the Abbey at Poissy |

| | |
|---|---|
| 1419 | Murder of John "the Fearless," duke of Burgundy at the hands of one of Charles' knights; Philip "the Good," becomes duke and allies himself with the English |
| 1419 | Burgundians take Paris, Dauphin in exile (with Jean de Castel) |
| 1422 | Death of Charles VI, Charles VII becomes king of France |
| | Death of Henry V, Henry VI becomes king of England and nominally king of France |
| 1425 | Death of Christine's son, Jean de Castel |
| 1429 | July 17, Coronation of Charles VII |
| 1429 | *The Tale of Joan of Arc* (*La Ditié de Jeanne d'Arc*) |
| 1431 | February 21, trial of Joan of Arc, execution follows, May 30, 1431 |
| 1434 | Death of Christine de Pizan before 1434 |

# Bibliographical note

Details about the life of Christine de Pizan, a complete list of her works, and her place within French culture and history can be found in Charity Canon Willard's *Christine de Pizan, Her Life and Works* (Persea Books, 1984).

There is no complete edition of Christine de Pizan's voluminous writings either in French or English. For those most interested in her political thought, *The Book of the City of Ladies* (trans. E. J. Richards [Persea Books, 1982]) and *A Medieval Woman's Mirror of Honor: The Treasury of the City of Ladies* (trans. C. C. Willard [Persea Books, 1989]) are highly recommended. In French, *Le Livre de la Paix*, ed. C. C. Willard (The Hague, 1958) and *Le Livre des Fais et des Bonnes Meurs du Sage Roy Charles V*, ed. Suzanne Solente (H. Champion, 1936-41) will be of great interest.

There have been very few studies of Christine de Pizan's politics and political thought. Two works by Diane Bornstein are useful. "Humanism in Christine de Pizan's Livre du Corps de Policie" (*Les Bonne Feuilles*, 3 (1975), 100–115) discusses Christine's use and understanding of her sources, while *Mirrors of Courtesy* (Archon Books, 1975) shows the place of her works within the traditional genre intended for the aristocracy. More recently, *Gender, Genre, and the Politics of Christine de Pizan* (ed. Margaret Brabant [Westview Press, 1992]) includes a number of very helpful essays. Among them is Sheila Delaney's provocative "Mothers to Think Back Through: Who Are They? The Ambiguous Example of Christine de Pizan" which has inspired considerable debate on Christine's role as a feminist writer. Christine Reno's "Christine de Pizan: At Best a Contra-

xxix

dictory Figure?" criticizes Delaney's position. My own essay "Poly-
cracy, Obligation, and Revolt: The Body Politic in John of Salisbury
and Christine de Pizan" shows how Christine's use of the corporate
metaphor she found in John's *Policraticus* reflects her very different
perception of political life.

Art historian Sandra Hindman's *Christine de Pizan's "Epistre
d'Othéa"; Painting and Politics at the Court of Charles VI* (Toronto,
1986) brings the insights of her discipline to the problem of reception.
She argues that illuminations can reveal an author's view of the changing politics of her audience.

General introductory works on medieval political thought abound.
Antony Black's *Political Thought in Europe 1250–1450* (Cambridge
University Press, 1992) is the best, providing depth of scholarship in
a very readable format. For an overview of the Hundred Years War,
Christopher Dyer's *The Age of Plantagenet and Valois* (New York,
1962) and Robin Neillands *The Hundred Years War* (Routledge, 1990)
are very useful for the undergraduate. Both provide a sense of the
dynastic and political issues at stake in this dramatic conflict. For
general background the *Cambridge History of Medieval Political Thought*
(ed. J. H. Burns [Cambridge University Press, 1988]) is the standard
if rather too conventional reference. Regrettably, it has very few references to "mirrors for princes" as a genre of political writing. For
that, we turn to French scholars: Dora Bell's *L'Idéal Ethique de la
Royauté en France au Môyen Age* (Droz, 1962) and Jacques Krynen's
*Idéal du Prince et du Pouvoir Royal en France à la Fin du Môyen Age*
(Picard, 1981).

For a sense of the general intellectual context out of which late
medieval political thought comes, C. S. Lewis' classic *The Discarded
Image* (Cambridge University Press, 1964) introduces the reader to
the mental framework that was the backdrop for didactic writing in
the Middle Ages. This world view is complemented by several other
works: George Duby's *The Three Orders* (University of Chicago Press,
1982), R. R. Bolgar's *Classical Influence on European Culture*
(Cambridge University Press, 1971), and Brian Stock's *The Implications of Literacy* (Princeton University Press, 1982). These books provide a sense of medieval culture in general, which by Christine's age
was believed to be disintegrating rapidly. A sense of cultural disorder
haunted many writers of this era, many of whom believed reform in
the character of princes was the only solution to political problems

since long established institutions seemed to be failing. This sense of disintegration and the new ways of looking at political problems ushered in as a result are explored in Quentin Skinner's *The Foundations of Modern Political Thought*, Vol. 1, *The Renaissance* (Cambridge University Press, 1978).

The idea of the Body Politic is classically addressed in E. Kantorwicz *The King's Two Bodies* (Princeton University Press, 1957). This seminal but now dated work should be supplemented by a number of articles by Cary J. Nederman (translator of the *Policraticus* in this series) especially "The Physiological Significance of the Organic Metaphor in John of Salisbury's *Policraticus*" (History of Political Thought, 7, no. 2 [Summer 1987]) which deals explicitly with the metaphor's usefulness in demonstrating interdependence as well as hierarchy. I also highly recommend Amnon Linder's "Knowledge of John of Salisbury in the later Middle Ages" (*Studii Medievali*, series 3, 18 [1977]). On the question of John of Salisbury and tyrannicide, see also my own 'Salisburian Stakes: The Uses of "Tyranny" in the *Policraticus*' (*History of Political Thought*, 11, no. 3 [Autumn 1990]) may be useful.

Those interested in the broader question of Christine's role in the history of feminism or of French literature are advised to consult Willard's *Christine de Pizan* for its excellent bibliography as well as Edith Yenal, *Christine de Pizan: A Bibliography of Writings* (Scarecrow Press, 1989).

In addition to the works listed here, the reader is urged to examine Plutarch's *Lives*, Livy's *History of the Romans*, and other classical historians, for alternative versions of the stories that Christine uses. These are readily available in modern editions.

# Glossary

## General note on medieval names

Medieval names are confusing to the modern reader since they were not as systematic or regular as our names are today. For example, a person's Christian name, received at baptism, could be followed by a variety of what we would call surnames or last names. Sometimes these were place names, referring to an individual's place of birth (John of Salisbury, Isabel of Bavaria), or a family's geographical origins (Christine de Pizan), and could change if the person's location changed. But names could also refer to a position held. Thus Philip of Harvengt's name refers to his birth place but later becomes Philip of Bonne Esperance, the abbey of which he was in charge. Names could even refer to a physical characteristic. Although Charles the Bald, Philip the Bold, and Charles the Fat were all kings, common names like Leroux, White, or Black also referred to physical characteristics. Christine de Pizan herself is sometimes referred to as Christine du Castel, from her husband's name. Pizan, which refers to the family's origins in Pizzano, is also sometimes spelled Pisan, as though she were from Pisa.

The names of commoners could be equally confusing. They might refer to an occupation, or a family's traditional work (John Fletcher, Alice Cooper, Adam Smith), to a place (Thomas of London), to a physical characteristic (Jack White), or to parentage (Thomas Williamson or Thomas Fitzwilliam). As a general rule of thumb, when looking for a shorter form of the name, if the name has an "of" referring to a place, the person is called by the Christian name.

# Glossary

John of Salisbury is called "John" by scholars, Christine de Pizan is "Christine." If there is a true surname, then the last name may be used, e.g. Thomas Becket can be "Becket," but John of Salisbury is never "Salisbury," always John! The exception that proves the rule is in noble titles: the earl of Salisbury, the king of France, the duke of Burgundy could indeed be referred to as Salisbury, France, Burgundy, but this usage is less common.

**advocate**   A university trained lawyer. The Advocates of Parliament were the most prestigious, and served as a council to the king, sometimes in opposition to the Estates General.

**Alcibiades** (450 BC–404 BC)   Athenian general and statesman, brilliant ambitious pupil of Socrates.

**Alexander** (the Great) (356 BC–323 BC)   Heroic soldier, general, and strategist from Macedonia, he was the conqueror of the "known world" and died at the age of thirty-three. His father, Philip of Macedon, hired the Greek philosopher Aristotle to be his tutor. Alexander was an inspiration to political and military leaders for hundreds of years.

**Anacharsis** (fl.*c.*600 BC)   Philosopher. This quotation comes from Plutarch's *Life of Solon*.

**Anaxagoras** (*c.*500 BC–*c.*428 BC)   Greek philosopher, very much admired by Aristotle.

**Antiochus** (the Great) (242 BC–187 BC)   King of Syria, Antiochus was defeated by Scipio Africanus Major and his brother Lucius at Magnesia in 190 BC.

**Apollo**   Greek god of the sun, music, and the healing arts, twin of the goddess Diana.

**Archimedes** (287 BC–212 BC)   Mathematician and inventor killed at the siege of Syracuse in modern day Sicily.

**Aristotle** (384 BC–322 BC)   Born in Stagira, tutor to Alexander the Great, student of Plato. "The Philosopher" wrote numerous works on politics, ethics, science and metaphysics that profoundly shaped Western political, moral, and scientific thinking.

**authors**   The authors (Greek and Roman philosophers, poets, historians) were the major authorities of the Middle Ages.

**Averroës** (AD 1126–98)   Islamic philosopher, translator of Aristotle.

**beatings**   Although this account of medieval education sounds quite harsh, it is actually quite "progressive" given the educational practices of the age. It is perhaps worth remembering that children were physically punished in schools in Europe and the Americas until very recently.

**Bodily ease**   This passage refers to a popular misconception about Epicurean philosophy, that is, that it preaches pleasure before all else.

**Boethius** (Anicius Manlius Severinus) (AD 480–524)   Considered a model statesman and philosopher throughout the Middle Ages. A major source in the transmission of classical philosophy, mathematics and science, he also wrote on mathematics and music. He was a statesman under the Ostrogoth Emperor of Rome, Theodoric. Imprisoned by Theodoric, he wrote his Consolation of Philosophy while awaiting his fate, and was later executed.

**Bretons**   Inhabitants of Brittany, Celtic enclave in north-western France.

**Burgundians**   Inhabitants of Burgundy, province in eastern France.

**Cannae**   Site of a battle between Carthage and Rome in 216 BC.

**Carneades** (*c.*214 BC–129 BC)   Philosopher and founder of the new Academy.

**Cato** (Marcus Porcius Cato) (234 BC–149 BC)   Considered the father of Roman prose. After an active political career, characterized by his advocacy of traditional values, Cato began to write history and an encyclopedia of practical information, among other works. The quotation here probably comes from a work attributed to Cato, written in the third century AD.

**Cleanthes** (331 BC–232 BC)   Greek disciple of Zeno, head of the Stoic school of philosophy from 263 BC to 232 BC.

**consul**   Roman political office. Under the republic, it was the supreme civil and military magistrature but during the imperial period it became an honorific. Christine's comparisons of Roman political life with that of her contemporaries typify the medieval desire to equate the two societies in many ways.

**Cyrus (I)** (fl.*c.*550 BC)   Wise and tolerant King of Persia.

**Darius (I)** (521 BC–486 BC)   King of Persia, fought the battle of Marathon.

**Darius (II)** (*c.*380–330 BC)   Fought against Alexander the Great.

**dart**   Short javelin-like weapon.

**decade**   Titus Livius' *History of the Romans* is in groups of ten books, referred to as "decades." Christine means books 21–30 in her reference to her source.

**Demades** (fl.350 BC–319 BC) Athenian politician.

**demesne** The central portion of the manor or estates of king or nobleman reserved for personal, household use.

**Democritus** (*c.*460 BC) The "laughing philosopher," scientist, mathematician opposed by the Stoics, Plato and Aristotle. His most famous students were Epicurus and Lucretius.

**Denis** (Dionysius I) (*c.*430 BC–367 BC) Tyrant of Syracuse.

**Diana** Roman goddess of the moon and the hunt, she is the twin of Apollo.

**dictator** From the Latin *dicere,* "to say."

**discord** A possible reference to the Great Schism.

**Emilius Lepidus** (Marcus Emilius Lepidus) (d.152 BC).

**Emilius Paulus** (Lucius Emilius Paulus) (d.*c.*160 BC).

**Euclid** (fl.*c.*300 BC) Greek mathematician, taught at Alexandria in present day Egypt.

**Epaminondas** (d.362 BC) Greek military and political leader from Thebes.

**estates** The basic idea of "estates" of the realm comes from the division into three major classes of medieval society: those who pray, those who fight and those who work – clergy, nobles, and commons. As political expression and participation became increasingly formalized and institutionalized, each "estate" or class was given a formal role. Clergy, nobles and commons were first summoned by Philip IV in 1304. Usually the Estates General were assembled in time of emergency in support of the monarchy.

**Euripides** (*c.*500 BC) Greek playwright.

**Fabricius** (Gaius Luscinus Fabricius) (fl.*c.*280 BC) Hero of war with Pyrrhus, Cicero describes him with Marcus Curius Denatus as typical of Roman virtues.

**Florus** (Lucius Annaeus Florus) (*c.*120 BC) Roman historian, rhetor, poet.

**fortune** Fortune was the goddess of chance, who by spinning her wheel, changed lives. Christine examines the idea of fortune in several of her books, especially *The Mutability of Fortune.*

**gentle** Member of a family in which the men bear arms by inheritance or grant, from Latin *gens, gentiles.*

**grammar** Medieval education consisted of the seven liberal arts, divided into the trivium (grammar, dialectic or logic, rhetoric) and the quadrivium (arithmetic, astronomy, geometry, music).

**Gyges** (*c.*685 BC–657 BC).

**habits**  From the Latin *habitus*. Habitually proper outward behavior – good manners – was believed to lead to a virtuous character. This Aristotelian theory of moral behavior was the cornerstone of medieval ethical thought.

**Hannibal** (247 BC–182 BC)  Military leader from Carthage, in North Africa. A great soldier, tactician, strategist, political reformer, he committed suicide rather than surrender to the Romans.

**Hector**  Semi-mythical prince and hero of Troy, in Homer's *Illiad*. Both Romans and French believed they were descendants of the Trojans; one of the reasons that Virgil's epic poem, *The Aeneid*, was much admired.

**Holy Spirit**  The third person of the Christian Trinity, the Holy Spirit is the aspect of God that inspires and encourages the individual.

**Hours**  Religious services corresponding to the hours of the monastic day, traditionally beginning with Matins at midnight, and followed by Lauds (dawn), Prime (6 am), Terce (9 am), Sext (noon), None (3 pm), Vespers (6 pm), and ending with Compline. By the late Middle Ages the Hours varied somewhat by location and customary usage: Matins and Lauds might be said together at midnight or at dawn, Prime and Terce combined before Mass, for example. But the rhythm of the day and of the seasons was punctuated by these prayers ideally to be heard or said by all Christians. Prayerbooks to guide non monastic participants began to develop in the fourteenth century, as non-monastic society became increasingly literate. Known as Books of Hours, they were sometimes sumptuously illustrated and, by the fifteenth century, were increasingly associated with private devotions and meditation.

**humors**  The four humors were the cornerstone of medieval medicine. The four elements (fire, air, water, earth) combined in different blends to make the four humors: hot and moist make blood; hot and dry, choler; cold and moist, phlegm; cold and dry, melancholy. Different mixtures (*temperatio*) shape the individual person's temperament. A lack of balance resulted in illness or predisposition to certain kinds of personality. An excess of choler (yellow bile) was associated with irritability and anger, phlegm with lethargy and obesity, blood made one warm and generous,

# Glossary

black bile (melancholer) was associated with depression and sadness. Each humor was associated with an organ which was influenced by an astrological sign and ruled by a planet. Thus the sanguine personality, – warm, generous, hot-tempered – was associated with Jupiter, the sign Leo, the heart, and blood. Many words we use today are have their origins in these medicalastrological theories: jovial, sanguine, melancholy, choleric, phlegmatic, hearty, and temper, for example.

**Isidore** (AD 560–636) Bishop of Seville, he was an influential writer, and churchman. His *Etymologies*, a source book and encyclopedia that was widely used, dates from *c.*630.

**Julius Caesar** (100 BC–44 BC) Roman hero, military general, ruler, named dictator for life in 44 BC, which led to his murder.

**Justin** (Marcus Junianius Justinus) (*c.*AD 300) Historian, widely read in the Middle Ages.

**Juvenal** (Decimus Lunius Juvenalis) (*c.*AD 60–*c.*140) Satirist and poet who was said to be exiled from court for his satire.

**Lacedemonia** Ancient name for the city of Sparta in Greece.

**Lycurgus** Semi-mythical Spartan leader *c.*800 BC.

**Lucan** (Marcus Annaeus Lucanus) (AD 39–65) Roman knight, brother of Seneca, his work is especially strong on the Roman civil war.

**manners** Manners were considered an important part of behavior because they reflected and taught good morals. See **habit**.

**Marathon** *C.*490 BC site of the famous battle between the Spartans and the Persians.

**Marcus Marcellus** (Marcus Claudius Marcellus) (fl.*c.*220 BC) Military hero of the first Punic War.

**Mars** Roman god of war.

**Mass** The most important public Catholic Christian worship service. The name comes from the Latin closing of the Mass, "Ite missa est."

**mirror** The idea of the mirror is an important one in medieval thought. The individual's most important duty in life was to imitate or mirror Christ.

**Mithridates** (Eupator Dionysius) (120 BC–63 BC)

**morals** See **habit**.

**Normans** Inhabitants of Normandy, descendants of Viking "Northmen," in northern France.

**Orosius Paulus** Pupil of St. Augustine, Historian *c.*AD 417.

**Ovid** (Publius Ouidius Naso) (430 BC–AD 17) Roman Poet. His *Metamorphoses* was an influential poem describing famous persons and events.

**Pericles** (*c.*495 BC–429 BC) Athenian statesman, described by Thucydides and Plutarch, known for his eloquence.

**Perses** King of Macedon (r.179 BC–168 BC)

**Pisistratus** (fl.*c.*670 BC) Tyrant of Athens, opposed by Solon.

**Plutarch** (*c.*AD 50–AD 120) Greek moralist and biographer, tutor to Emperor Trajan. His *Lives* was a well-known source of *exempla*, and he was much admired as the teacher of the most revered Roman emperor.

**Pompey** the Great (Gnaeus Pompeius) (106 BC–48 BC) Roman general and statesman, member of the first triumvirate after the death of Julius Caesar.

**prebend** Medieval clerics were not paid formal salaries for their duties. Instead they were furnished with income from lands which the church or cathedral owned.

**price** Once captured by the enemy, one's only hope of returning home again was through either a treaty or ransom. In a society that set great importance on rank, ransom was set according to one's worth in the social system, that is, a baron had a higher price than a knight, a knight required a higher ransom than a footsoldier, who would be lucky if his family would ransom him at all. Thus a soldier of no price was one who could not be exchanged for ransom.

**prince** Comes from the Latin word *princeps*, "first," and referred not only to a king's son, but could mean any high ranking ruler; a bishop, king, Pope, duke, etc.

**Ptolemy** (Claudius Ptolemaeus) (fl.AD 127–48) Astronomer and mathematician. His ideas dominated the study of astronomy for 1,500 years.

**Pyrrhus** (319 BC–272 BC) Most famous Molossian King of Epirus. The terrible price he paid for his victory in the battle against the Romans at Asculum in 279 BC that Christine describes is the source of the expression "pyrrhic victory."

**Pythagoras** (*c.*531 BC) Greek philosopher and mathematician.

**rank** Medieval society had strict rules of precedence, and movement from one class to another was not easy. Rank determined dress, income, style of life, education. The ambitious might try to learn the manners of another class in order to become more mobile. In Christine's day, the emergence of a middle class that was educated and fairly well off challenged a society which only semi-officially recognized any classes other than clergy, nobles, and peasants – "Those who pray, those who fight, and those who work."

**ransom** Once captured by the enemy, one's only hope of returning home again was either through a treaty or ransom. In a society that set great importance on rank, ransom was set according to one's worth in the social system, that is, a baron had a higher price than a knight, a knight required a higher ransom than a footsoldier, who would be lucky if his family would ransom him at all.

**rule of life** Originally an idea from the monastic world. Every person ought to have a rule of life governing his or her circumstances, responsibilities and behavior.

**Saint Anselm** (AD 1033–1109) Archbishop of Canterbury, one of the most influential philosophers of the Middle Ages.

**Saint Augustine** (AD 354–430) The towering figure of Augustine of Hippo was to influence philosophy, history, and literature for a thousand years. He was born in Tagaste, North Africa, son of a pagan father and Christian mother (Saint Monica). His pagan upbringing, his wild youth, his devotion to philosophy, and ultimate conversion to Christianity have inspired generations of readers. A prolific writer, his *Confessions* (an autobiography) and *The City of God*, are his two most famous works.

**Saint Matthew** Early Jewish follower of Jesus, wrote a "gospel" or life of the sayings and teachings of Jesus.

**Saint Paul** A Roman citizen, Paul was an early follower of Jesus. Known especially for his letters (Epistles) considered part of the Christian Bible.

**Saint Peter** Leader of the followers of Jesus after his crucifixion. Believed to have been the first Pope.

**Sallust** (Gaius Sallustius) (*c*.86 BC–35 BC) Served as a tribune and in the Roman Senate. After an active political life, he retired to write history.

**Sappho** (*c*.612 BC) Greek poet from the island of Lesbos. While Christine knew that Sappho was a woman, in the fifteenth century Sappho was not yet associated with homosexuality.

**science**  From the Latin *scientia* "knowledge," it was a much broader term than it is today, having a meaning closer to learning or scholarship.

**Scipio Africanus Major** (236 BC–184 BC)  Military strategist and hero.

**Scipio Africanus Minor** (185 BC–129 BC)  Politician, general, Cicero's model statesman-philosopher.

**Scipio Nasica Publius Cornelius** (*c.*160 BC)  Learned in law, he upheld traditional standards of morality and politics.

**Seneca** (Lucius Annaeus Seneca) (*c.*4 BC–AD 65)  Stoic writer and philosopher, teacher of Emperor Nero. During Seneca's life, he was able to keep Nero somewhat under control, but after Nero forced Seneca to commit suicide, his cruelty went unchallenged. In the Middle Ages, he was widely admired and quoted. Martin of Braga's *Formula Honestae Vitae* was believed to have been written by Seneca, and was often quoted in mirrors for princes, including Christine's *Livre de prudence* and Walter de Milemete's *De nobilitatibus*.

**Sertorius** (Quintus Sertorius) (d.*c.*73 BC)  Heroic Roman soldier who opposed both the dictator Sulla and his general, Pompey.

**servitude**  Christine is referring here to the complex social relationships of the Middle Ages. To owe a tax entailed a different (and lower) social relation from that of a person who gave money more or less freely to an overlord. Christine seeks to reassure those who feared a loss of social status by paying taxes.

**sheep**  Christine's use of this metaphor reflects both Scriptural sources and her own knowledge. One of her earliest works was *The Shepherdess*.

**simple**  humble, lower class, not eligible to bear arms.

**Solinus** (Gaius Iulius Solinus) (*c.*AD 200)  Historian and geographer. The first source to refer to the Mediterranean Sea. Most of his material comes from Pliny.

**Solon** (fl.*c.*600 BC)  Athenian statesman and legislator. One of the "Seven Sages."

**sovereign**  Literally, to rule over; could refer to a nation, an area, or oneself.

**tables**  Historically, tables were not permanent fixtures in aristocratic dining halls because the space was too valuable and the numbers of people too unpredictable to justify them. Instead, trestles with boards across them were set up and taken down before and after meals. This custom is the source of the expression "room and board." Notice Christine assumes that the Romans had the same custom and that the tables of those of lower rank would be put away first, as in her own time.

**Tarquin** (Tarquinius Superbus) (Traditional dates 534 BC–510 BC) Semi-legendary last king of Rome.

**Thales** (fl.580 BC) Greek philosopher and one of the "Seven Sages," considered the founder of geometry and physical science.

**Themistocles** (c.528 BC–462 BC) Athenian democratic statesman.

**Tiberias** (42 BC–AD 37) Emperor of the Romans.

**Tigranes** (d.c.56 BC) Allied with Mithridates, defeated 66 BC.

**Titus** (Titus Flavius Vespasianus) (AD 39–81) Emperor of Rome AD 79–81, deified after his death.

**Titus Livius** (Livy) (59 BC–AD 17 or 64 BC–12 AD) Roman historian. His *History of the Romans* contained 142 books of which 35 are still extant. Although he was uncritical of his sources, the history is vividly and graphically written.

**Tully** (Marcus Tullius Cicero) (106 BC–AD 43) Model for the Middle Ages of the statesman-philosopher.

**Valerius** (Valerius Maximus) (c.AD 20) Wrote a history of the "memorable deeds and words" of the Romans dedicated to Emperor Tiberius. His sources include Livy, Cicero, Varro, Trogus Pompeius. His compilation was widely admired and used during the Middle Ages as a source of *exempla*.

**Varro** (Marcus Tarentius) (116 BC–27 BC) Roman librarian, writer, editor, historian, scientist. Wrote at least fifty-five works of which we have only two today.

**Vegetius** (Renatus Flavius Vegetius) (fl.AD 380) A bureaucrat, but neither historian nor soldier, his *Epitome Rei Militaris* is not necessarily accurate about Roman military history but was very influential.

**Vesta** Roman Goddess of the hearth.

**Volscii** Inhabitants of the central part of the Italian peninsula, Latinium.

**Xerxes** Persian Emperor 486 BC–465 BC, son of Darius I.

# THE BOOK OF THE
# BODY POLITIC

PART ONE

# On Princes

Here begins the Book of the Body Politic which speaks of virtue and manners* and is divided into three parts. The first part is addressed to princes,* the second to knights and nobles, and the third to the universal people.

## Chapter 1 The first chapter gives the description of the Body Politic

If it is possible for vice to give birth to virtue, it pleases me in this part to be as passionate as a woman, since many men assume that the female sex does not know how to silence the abundance of their spirits. Come boldly, then and be shown the many inexhaustible springs and fountains of my courage, which cannot be stanched when it expresses the desire for virtue.

Oh, Virtue, noble and godly, how can I dare to flaunt myself by speaking of you, when I know that my understanding neither comprehends nor expresses you well?

But what comforts me and makes me bold is that I sense that you are so kind that it will not displease you if I speak of you, not about what is most subtle, but only in those areas which I can conceive or comprehend. So, I will speak about you as far as it concerns the teaching of good morals, by speaking first of the industry and rule of life* for our superiors; that is, princes, whose majesties I humbly supplicate not to take wrongly nor disdain such a small intelligence as mine, that such a humble creature dares undertake to speak about the way of life for higher ranks.* And may it please them to remember the teaching of the Philosopher, who said, "Do not disdain the wise words of the insignificant despite your own high position." Next, by the grace of God, I hope to speak on the manner of life of knights and nobles. And then, thirdly, on the whole universal people.

These three types of estate ought to be one polity like a living body according to the words of Plutarch* who in a letter which he sent to the Emperor Trajan compared the polity to a body having life. There the prince and princes hold the place of the head in as much as they are or should be sovereign* and from them ought to come particular institutions just as from the mind of a person springs forth the external deeds that the limbs achieve. The knights and nobles take the place of the hands and arms. Just as a person's arms have to be strong in order to endure labor, so they have the burden of defending the law of the prince and the polity. They are also the hands because, just as the hands push aside harmful things, so they ought push all harmful and useless things aside. The other kinds of people are like the belly, the feet, and the legs. Just as the belly receives all that the head and the limbs prepare for it, so, too, the activity of the prince and nobles ought to return to the public good, as will be better explained later. Just as the legs and feet sustain the human body, so, too, the laborers sustain all the other estates.*

## Chapter 2 Which describes how virtuous felicity is symbolized

First we have to discuss virtue, to the benefit of the rule of life for the three different estates. Virtue must regulate human life in all its works. Without it, no one can have honor. Whatever the degree of honor, Valerius* says, honor is the plentiful food of virtue. And on this subject, Aristotle* said, "Reverence is due to honor as a testimony of virtue," which means that honor must not be attributed but to a virtuous person, because he is not speaking about the powerful nor about the rich, but the virtuous. According to him, only the good are honored. Nothing is more desired by noble hearts than honor. As he says himself in the fourth book of the *Ethics*, neither power nor riches is without honor. Now it is true that kings and powerful princes are especially invested with honor, and as a consequence, virtue, so it is appropriate to distinguish the aspects of virtue. In chapter 20 of his book, *The City of God*, St. Augustine* says that the philosophers say that virtue is the objective of all human good and evil. That is, human happiness comes from being virtuous.

Now it is fitting that there is great delight in happiness, otherwise it would not be happiness, and this joy and happiness ancient philosophers described and symbolized in this manner: Felicity is a very beautiful and refined queen seated on a royal throne, and the virtues are seated around her and look at her, waiting to hear her commands, to serve her, and to obey. She commands Prudence to inquire how she can stay healthy and in good condition so that she can reign a long time. And she commands Justice to do everything that she should and keep the laws so that there will be peace. And she commands Courage that if any pain should come to her body, to moderate it by resisting it with virtuous thought. She commands Temperance to take wine, food and other delectable things in moderation so that anything she takes is for a reason and not to her detriment. This description allows one to understand that to be virtuous is nothing more than to have in one everything that attracts good and which pushes away evil and vice. Thus, in order to govern the body of the public polity well, it is necessary for the head to be healthy, that is, virtuous. Because if it is ill, the whole body will feel it. Therefore we begin by speaking of medicine for the head, that is, for the king or princes, and, since this is a work beginning with the head, we will take first the "head" of age, that is the childhood of the prince who is brought up on the responsibility of his parents.

## Chapter 3 This tells how one ought to bring up the children of princes

Because we are expressly commanded to love God, the first thing is to introduce the child of the prince to this love very early and to teach him simple little prayers appropriate to the understanding of the child.

For things taught early in childhood are lost with difficulty. Such things are agreeable to God; the Psalmist says "The Lord has perfect praise in the mouth of children and sucklings," that is, He approves of it. As he gets older he should learn his letters and to follow the religious service. God be praised, to teach their children to hear

Mass* and to say their Hours* has been the praiseworthy custom of the princes of France more than in other places.

Also one ought to provide a tutor who is wise and prudent more in morals than in lofty learning, despite the fact that in ancient times, the children of princes were taught by philosophers. For example, Philip, king of Macedon and father of the great Alexander,* wrote to Aristotle that while he had had great joy when a male infant was born to him, he had a greater joy yet that he was born at this time so that he could be instructed and taught by Aristotle who eventually was the teacher of Alexander the Great. Nevertheless, because at present princes do not desire to be educated in the sciences* as they used to be and as I would wish it pleased God that they were, I believe that it would be better to have a very discrete and wise tutor, who had good morals and loved God, rather than the most excellent and subtle philosopher. Yet it would be much more praiseworthy to find a perfect one who was a notable scholar as well.

And so princes ought to carefully search for one because the good morals that the child sees in his tutor, and the wise words and countenance he experiences provide both an education and a mirror* for him. So the wise tutor ought to conduct himself with great prudence in such an office, because despite the fact that it is a child's nature not to learn except out of fear of punishment, nevertheless, it is good that the child of the prince be brought to fear in other ways than severe beatings.* For too strict a correction in a child that is brought up in pleasures and who already senses the power of authority because of the honor that others pay him could lead, instead of to correction, to indignation towards learning as well as towards his tutor, which would undermine his discipline, to the detriment of the tutor and, perhaps, of the health of the delicately raised child. But what should the wise tutor do? He ought to follow the example of the lion, because it is the custom to raise the children of princes with other children, sons of barons, who are all his pupils. He ought to be severe with them when they misbehave and beat them as is customary but threaten them more by severe expression than by beatings, and likewise to use threats on the prince's son if he does not correct himself. At some point, let him feel the rod, and by this see to it that he is ashamed of his misdeed, fearful, and obedient.

The wise tutor ought not to be too familiar with or too close to his pupils because they will fear him less, and the child should not

6

see him play games, laugh, or speak foolishly, but, instead that he is not too familiar with anyone but is half school master to everyone. And his countenance should be dignified and firm, and his dress be clean and honorable. In front of his pupil, he should not speak empty words but profitable ones, and give good examples; however, he should not always have a sour face and proud words. He ought to welcome him with gentle words when he does well which will reward him if he does something good. The master shall give him these little things that delight children, or sometimes tell him childish stories or something that makes them laugh. The purpose of all that is that he love his tutor as well as his studies. The master should regulate the day well, and arrange time and rules for the child to begin and end school, and then give him some time to play before his dinner, which should be orderly, and not too rich or delicate in meats and wines, which to some degree can cause corruption or illness. And when the child comes to learn his grammar* then the tutor should begin to use a bit more subtle words and teaching, according to how he sees what the child is able to understand, and thus, little by little, teach more and more, just as a nurse increases the food of the child according to his growth.

Truly, I believe that the prince would want to have his child to be introduced to learning so that he knows the rules of grammar and understands Latin, which if pleased God, I would wish were generally the custom for all children of princes at present and for the future, because I believe that the greater good would ensue and virtue would increase for them and their subjects. So they should have their children learn as much as possible, to advance as far as Logic, and then have them continue if they can. So the very wise prince, the duke of Orleans, did and used to do for his children, as he was asked by the very wise, good, and virtuous duchess, his wife, who values and honors education and knowledge, and like a prudent mother is careful that letters and all the virtues are being learned by her children.

With the wise tutor described above, when the understanding of the child begins to grow and to understand better, then he ought to feed him more advanced learning and manners by giving him examples or having him read in books. And he ought to make him understand the difference between good and evil, and teach and show him the path to follow in good morals, manners, and virtue as the valiant and renowned princes, his predecessors, and others did, and show him the great good which comes from being good and governing oneself well, and also the opposite; the evil which comes to the bad or vicious. And if he seems at all inclined or talented in learning, he ought to encourage him through pleasant words and reasons, so that he will understand the great happiness to be found in learning, opening up for him the path to philosophy, and making him appreciate and understand it. And if he has such a tutor at the beginning, if he continues with such learning when he comes of age the son of the prince will have excellence in virtue and great fame.

## Chapter 4 On the sort of person to be entrusted with the governing of the children of princes

When the son of the prince has grown older, then he ought to be separated from the women who have cared for him and his care ought to be entrusted principally to one older knight of great authority, and one ought to carefully look to see that he is wise, loyal, prudent, and of good manner of life, and that he have similar persons around him. This knight must take as much or more diligent care of the habits* of the child as he does of his body. So he ought to take care that he rises early; that he hears Mass, says his Hours, has a pleasant and confident expression, speaks well to people, greets them kindly, gives to everyone the honor due to his position. This knight ought often to show him what the honor and valor of knighthood is, and tell him the great deeds of many worthy knights. He ought to make him recognize who is good and who is the better in his father's household and who he ought to honor the most. And he ought to show him and teach him the emblems of arms and order of battles and chivalry, how to fight, to attack, to defend, and for what quarrels one must take arms and fight, what armor is the best, strongest, and most sure, and most comfortable, and he ought to explain to him why it is so and how one should arm according to the kind of battle, what arms one would use, how one fought in times past and how now, how to determine who is good and worthy, and to attract them to oneself, to honor them, and to love them.

The knight ought to take care that there be neither great nor humble tellers of dishonest or evil ideas around the son of the prince when he has grown older, and that they not introduce the prince to folly. And he ought to take care that the children who are around him are well brought up, so that he is not induced to do wrong or to childish folly. If the child of the prince does wrong he should correct him, saying that it is not appropriate to his rank for the prince to do this, and that if he does not change he will encounter shame and blame, and that a prince without honor is worth nothing, and that if he does not desire to be governed this way, that he will have to leave. And thus he ought to counsel, tell, and admonish him often, and in this way the sons of princes and lords ought to be governed if they desire to be honorable in the future. Valerius affirms this for us in his book which speaks of how the ancients introduced the young to good manners, to withstand hardship, and to be honorable and brave. He told of the chivalry and bravery of the good, and gave good examples, telling them that nothing leads to honor as well as virtue.

At meals, he has songs sung about the deeds of the noble dead and the good deeds of their ancestors so that the will of the young person is made courageous. Valerius says that the ancients taught bravery, chivalry and good manners this way in their schools. These schools, he says, resulted in the Caesars and the noble families, renowned for accomplishments and bravery. And there is no doubt that good example and wise advice often heard and seen in childhood can cause a man to grow up excellent in all virtue, and similarly, by evil teaching one can be brought to the way of perdition. As Averroës* says in the second book of *Physics*, one can acquire a second nature by long habit of good or evil, and that is why parents ought to keep children from bad habits in youth as much as they can, for, says Orosius,* an earthenware pot keeps the odor of what it contained for a long time. It is because of this that the ancient Greeks who governed themselves with great learning and cleverness, took great pains to ensure that the people whom they hated delighted in evil habits, and this gave them the means to be avenged on them.

## Chapter 5 The exhortations that one ought to make to children of princes

While he is a child, the son of the prince also ought to be brought sometimes to the court, where the wise and the councillors* who determine the needs of the country are assembled, in order to hear the cases that come before them and the methods of good government of the polity, so that the child will be led to hear about the deeds and the governance of the realm that he is heir to, and will learn to speak about and to discuss these things. And the knights and the wise who are in the government ought to tell him to listen and remember what they say about this.

His guardians ought to speak in front of him about all kinds of unfamiliar things: different countries, the customs of warriors, battles, the rulers of many places, different weapons, and also the clergy, the Pope and the church. Theologians ought to speak to him about the law of the commandments and what one ought to hold and believe as a Christian, and sometimes he ought to hear sermons and reflections by clerics. He ought to hear sometimes about the common people, laborers, and merchants, how they make their profit from the poor and the rich, and similarly all kinds of things, so that his understanding is not found ignorant of anything that can be virtuously known. For the Philosopher says that he only is wise who understands everything. Also, it is good for him sometimes to exercise his body both in some work and in some suitable games like tennis and similar sports, but not too much, only so that he does not become too heavy and fat from too much rest, so that he accumulates superfluous humors.* Likewise one ought to speak to him about the poor and indigent and show them to him and tell him to have pity and compassion on them and do good to them for the love of God if he wants to gain paradise. Also that he should pity poor gentlewomen,* widows, and orphans and succor their needs for the love of God and out of kindness; and also all poor women and men in his power and to hear their requests kindly.

And one must teach him to be kind, humble, and truthful, tell him that despite that by the grace and will of God, he has been raised to high rank, he is as mortal as any other, and he will keep nothing with him but the good and evil that he has done, and that much is required from those given much. He ought not to be arrogant or proud in his heart, even though given great honors, but he should above all give thanks to God from whom the benefits he receives come, as he ought to recognize. Thus, he ought to hear many such admonishments to good and virtuous conduct. Yet despite this, one ought to allow the son of the prince to play and divert himself as mentioned before. And it must not be forgotten to encourage him in the virtues and in good manners.

## Chapter 6 Here it tells what the young prince should do when he begins to govern

When the time comes that the son of the prince has grown, and come of age to rule, and comes into his heritage by succession, whether it is a kingdom or another lordship, just as the fruit appears after the tree blossoms, so in him ought to appear the perfection of virtue, following the example of the wise king of France, Charles V. Because from the moment of his coronation, even though it was in the flower of his youth, no one could find anything dishonest in him and he occupied his time in suitable and virtuous things. I have plainly spoken elsewhere of him in my book on his deeds and good manners.

The virtues of a prince are seen in three things, without which he will not achieve this crown of reputation, good name, and consequently, honor. The first and most important, is to love, fear, and serve God without dishonesty, but with good deeds rather than spending time withdrawn in long prayers.

Another is this: he ought solely to love the good and benefit of his country and his people. All his ability, power, and the study of his free time ought to be for this, rather than his own benefit. The third is that he must love justice above all, guarding it and keeping it without restraint, and must do equity to all people. By keeping these three points well, the prince will be crowned with glory in heaven and on earth.

Now we will continue our work as before: Just as part I speaks of the head, that is the prince or princes, so we continue to discuss the first of our three points. From the first which is to love God, we will follow the many branches of virtue which stem from it, and likewise, the other two points.

## Chapter 7 The wise advice that is suitable for a young prince

The young prince who loves God will be afraid to do anything against His reverence and commandment, and will work hard to know everything that he ought to do and what he should avoid. Thus he will learn to perceive and comprehend his fragility as a mortal human, subject to a brief life, impassioned by transient mortal affairs and as frail as any other person, no different except for the gifts of fortune.*

But when he studies the law of God, in order to be well informed on it in like any good Christian ought to be, he will warn himself about the peril of these gifts for the soul, that is, if he does not use them properly, he is lost. The grandeur of lordship is only a transitory right of office of short duration and which he must leave in a brief time, that is, at death, which is a dark and painful thing. He will pay the accounts that he must render before the judge from whom nothing is hidden nor concealed, according to his merit. If the prince remembers this well, he will praise little those worldly goods and honors which are so perilous and short lived.

The good prince will have these thoughts in his heart; they will defend him against elevation of pride and lack of self-knowledge. However, God has chosen him for the burden of the office of rule, and he must maintain it in the world, by moral discretion. He then decides that he will live and govern by the laws of a prince of good habits and virtue, and will exercise his office to the best of his ability for the common good of his kingdom and country. Then he will judiciously use the magnificence and honors which the world delivers to him, and his heart will not be impeded nor raised against his God.

This good prince, as vicar of God on earth, will care with all his heart for the welfare of the church, so that his Creator can be served as his reason demands. And if there is any discord* through the instigation of the enemy, he will bring peace whatever the difficulty. He should examine carefully the promotions of the ministers, that he does not grant a request for a prebend,* no matter how much affection he has for the individual who requests it, unless he knows him to be a good and prudent cleric and fit to serve God and his service. And so the prince ought to examine carefully whether he should give the office or not, or else it will be a heavy burden on his conscience and the cause of the damnation of those he promotes, when given to those who do not deserve it, rather than as is described by decree.

But at present this rule is not followed, which is a pity, because God knows if sufficient worth and a just life are now the reason clerics are promoted. Certainly not; but rather promotions are given because of flattery, adulation, and other wickedness, by the requests of lords. Because of this, the ship is buffeted by the wind and ruined, because greed is the reason for their promotion. And even those in detestable and blind error are promoted, which continues even today in the church. Alas, as Jesus Christ said in the Gospel speaking to the Pharisees, "The queen of Sheba who came from far lands to see the wisdom of Solomon will condemn you. For you have with you one who is greater than Solomon, and you do not recognize it." Even the pagans of old held to their law without breaking it, carefully keeping it, observing all the ceremonies with great reverence, and yet this law was false and reproved by God. They are a reproach to Christians whose law has so much dignity and holiness yet is so badly kept and observed. Is it not written that the ancient pagans, who had great devotion to their idols and gods, were diligent and careful that the laws of their institutions were well kept, and that the priests who made the sacrifices were persons of good and honest life? And if they were not, they were severely punished, for they were so closely watched that they were not allowed to fail or to have vices.

In his first chapter, Valerius told that once in Rome a chaplet fell off when one of their priests was making a sacrifice. (A chaplet was a vestment they put on, like a mitre.) They believed that that meant he was negligent and not worthy of office, and they deposed him. Likewise, there was a maiden sent to the temple of one of their goddesses, called Vesta* (the maiden would be what we call a nun). She was negligent in caring for the lamp that was always kept lit, and was very severely punished, because she let the oil be used up, and she was deposed from office. And there are many more examples of this.

But there are enough of our bishops and priests who can be publicly seen in horrible faults. There is no prince nor other person who will reprove them, but they excuse themselves from what they are accused, by saying that they are human beings, not angels, and that it is human nature to sin. Alas! they are not human, because the body of a human is a little vessel which is filled by very little, but they are truly devils and the infernal abyss, for as the mouth of Hell may never be filled nor satisfied no matter how much it receives or takes, neither can their desires be satisfied or filled since they have such great greed in them for money and luxuries, for which they do great evil to the people! This is verified by the words of Valerius who asked "What thing will the avaricious not do in their insatiable hunger for gold?"

So the good prince ought to take care of all these things, because despite the fact that correction of people in the church is not his to undertake, nonetheless what prelate, priest, or cleric is so great that he will dare withstand or complain about the prince who reproves him for his manifest vice or sin? Moreover, the king or the good prince takes care that the temple and the house of God is not polluted nor profaned by the many sins committed there by many of our Christians nowadays; nobles, merchants, and people of every rank who are not ashamed to hold their meetings in churches, to have assemblies on their worldly affairs. They and God know what false contracts are made here.

Once Jesus Christ spoke of this in the Gospel when he said, "Would you make the temple of my father, which is a house of prayer, into a lair of thieves and a place of worldly things?" So the order which held among the ancient pagans condemns us. Valerius tells us about the devotion the Romans had to their gods, when he speaks of two consuls,* that is two princes and dukes of Rome, who were in a strange land with a great army. Because they consulted each other within the confines of the temple – nothing more – the Senate, that is the grand council* of rulers, deposed them from their office, despite the fact that they were very admirable men. It seems that one of the princes, whose name was Fabius Maximus, a marvelously brave man and chivalrous in fighting, was deposed from the highest office of prince the Romans had (which they called "dictator," because from all the other offices one could appeal to the dictator* according to their laws and statutes. But from the dictator one could not appeal to anyone else). He was deposed because he heard different cases in the temple. And for something like this they deposed Caius Flamius from his role, for he was a great military leader. Alas, no one is deposed nowadays; not only those who have meetings and parliaments in churches but make churches like foul stables for horses.

## Chapter 8 Of the observance towards God and toward the law which the prince ought to practice

The good prince who loves God will know his commandments by memory, and how the worthy name of God must not be taken in vain. To this purpose he will proclaim an edict throughout his land, which will forbid on pain of severe punishment anyone swearing on or denying his Creator. Alas, there is great need in France at present for such an edict, because it is horrible that the whole of Christendom has the custom of such disrespect toward the Savior. One can scarcely hear any other language, whether it be in jest or another manner of speech, but everyone swears horribly at every word about the torments of the passion of our redeemer, and they forsake and deny him. I believe that the pagans of old would not have treated their gods and idols so!

All these things the good prince ought to forbid, because they are opposed to and disapproved by the Christian religion and could be the cause of the wrath of God and the subversion of kingdoms and countries where they take place, as some prophesies tell. And so, the good prince who loves God will carefully observe and keep the divine law and holy institutions in everything that is worthy and devout (which I will not discuss for reasons of brevity, and also because most people would prefer to hear of less boring things). But the good prince that keeps and observes these things ought to believe firmly that God will guard, defend, and increase him in virtue of soul and body. And why should he not have faith in God, the living, all powerful, and just, whenever the pagans trusted that their needs would be met generously, because of the worship that they gave to their gods and their idols? It appears, by what Valerius says, that the city of Rome desired to serve the gods conscientiously, and he said, "Our city has always set aside everything for the service of the gods," even those things that concerned the honor of the sovereign majesty, that is, the emperors, because they had, he says, firm belief that in doing thus they acquired the rule and the governance of the world, and also because of this "the emperors of our city have generally not abandoned the constant service of holy things."

This suffices for the first point of the first part, on the virtue of the prince, which should to be founded on and should demonstrate the fact that he loves and serves God.

## Chapter 9 How a good prince ought to resemble a good shepherd

Now we have discussed the first point on which the goodness of the prince ought principally to be founded, so next we shall speak of the second point, that is, that the good prince ought especially to love the public good and its augmentation more than his own good, according to the teaching of Aristotle's *Politics*, which says that tyranny is when the prince prefers his own good over the public good. This is against royal lordship as well, for he ought to care more for the benefit of his people than his own. Now he shall be advised on how to demonstrate this love.

The good prince who loves his country will guard it carefully, following the example of the good shepherd. As he guards his sheep* from wolves and evil beasts, and keeps them clean and healthy so that they can increase and be fruitful and yield their fleece whole, sound, and well nourished by the land on which they are fed and kept, so that the shepherd will be well paid by their fleece, shorn in time and in season. But the rich good shepherd who gives them to others to keep because he cannot take care of all his flocks himself, provides himself with good and capable help. So he takes good, careful servants, wise and hard working in their craft, whom he understands and knows are loyal and prefer his interest. So he orders that those servants be equipped with good strong dogs with iron collars, well trained by being brought to the field to chase off wolves. So they let them loose at night in the fold so that thieves coming for the sheep are attacked by them. By day, they keep them tied to their belts while the sheep graze peacefully in the fields. But if these servants feel any fear of wolves or evil animals coming out of the woods or mountains, they then unleash the dogs, and let them run after them and nip at their heels. And to give the dogs greater boldness against the wolf or evil animal the servants run after them with good ironclad staffs. And if any sheep goes out of the flock, the good hounds go after it and, without doing it harm, they bring it back to the flock. In this manner, the wise servants defend and take care of them so well that they yield a good account to the head shepherd.

Just so, the good prince is mindful of the defense and care of his country and people, even though it is impossible in person. In every place he has responsibility, he will always provide himself with very good assistance, in deeds of knighthood and for other things; that is, the brave leaders whom he knows are good and loyal and who love him, such as constables, marshals, admirals and others, to whom he gives responsibility for furnishing other good soldiers, well-taught and experienced in war, whom he binds to him by an oath, not to leave without permission and are so ready to do his business that if needed they will go attack his enemies, so that the country is not despoiled, pillaged, nor the people killed. This does not mean that the soldiers themselves should pillage and despoil the country like they do in France nowadays when in other countries they dare not do so. It is a great mischief and perversion of law when those who are intended for the defense of the people, pillage, rob, and so cruelly, that truly short of killing them or setting their houses on fire, their enemies could do no worse. This is not the right manner of warfare, which ought to be just and without extortion, and if not, the soldiers and the princes that send them to war are in great peril of the wrath of God falling on them and punishing them severely. Before God, there is no doubt that the justifiable curses of the people, when they have been oppressed too much, can cause evil fortune to fall, as, for example, one finds in many places in Holy Scripture; for everyone ought to know that God is just, and all this is the fault of an evil order. For if soldiers were well paid, one could restrict them on pain of punishment to take nothing without paying for it, and by this means they could find provisions and everything that they needed economically and plentifully. It is too greatly astonishing how people can live under such a law without any compassion from the soldiers for the pity of their life. But the Holy Spirit,* father of the poor, will visit them! Now, if a shepherd had a dog that ran after his sheep, he would hit him with his staff. It is not a thing a good prince who loves God and his people should bear, and just as one unleashes the dogs at night in the fold to keep them from thieves, so must the head keep watchmen and spies along the borders so that the country and the people are not surprised by thieves or by some trickery, and so that they can know the plans of their enemies.

The soldiers ought to have yet another duty. Just as the good dog brings back the strayed sheep, so they ought to bring back the common people or others who from fear or dread or evil want to rebel and take the wrong side. They ought to bring them back to the right path either by threats or by taking good care of them. Although it displeases some and surprises others, I compare the noble office of arms to the nature of the dog because, truly, the dog naturally has many characteristics which the good man-at-arms ought to have. The dog loves his master marvelously and is very loyal to him. And the man-at-arms should be also. He is tough and exposes himself to death for his master and when he is committed to guarding any place he is very alert and has excellent hearing in order to run after evil doers or thieves. He will not bite the friends of his master but naturally sniffs at them, nor does he bite the neighbors nor those of the household where he is fed, but he guards them instead. He is very tough and fights with great skill. He has a good understanding, knowledge, and is very amiable to those who do him kindness. And all these characteristics are those of the good soldier.

## Chapter 10 On the same subject

Let us return to our first topic: the good shepherd who takes care that his sheep are well kept and healthy. The good prince will not put all his responsibilities onto his ministers, but will make himself available to his subjects so as to hear as many pleas as he can. He will not fear nor despise the pitiful supplications of the people, but kindly condescends to their requests for mercy and justice. So he takes care that they are not pressured more than is reasonable, nor "devoured" by bad ministers and officers.

To speak clearly on this would take great leisure and space and perhaps the truth will displease some; but without doubt, it is a great pity when the truth is quieted and muted either from fear or from favoritism. On this subject, Seneca* speaks in the sixth book in the twenty-first chapter of *On Benefices*. "I will show you," he says, "What those who are raised to high rank need most, although one thinks they have everything; that is, that someone would tell them the truth." This sentence is true because the servitors around princes do not seek their good but their individual benefit, and many of these tend to flatter and say what will please their lord and thus by their blandishments blind them. As it is written in chapter 15, book 3 of the *Politics*, the flatterer is the enemy of all virtues and he is a nail in the eye of his acquaintances. And on the subject of these officers, both the good and bad ones, without writing too much about them or about their deeds, I wish to God that princes studied who the people were they have around them, and who the people are that they have around them in the administration of their affairs, and knew their deeds well. For I believe that there is nothing more vile or corrupt than the conscience of some of them in their perversities.

But there are some of great evil and malice who conspire to hide their vices in darkness by coloring their virtues brightly. But they cannot hide the experiences others have of their deeds and words; as beautiful as they seem, there is no truth in them. They manifest

18

their iniquities to those who suffer at their hands. But this is not apparent to the lords before whom they dissimulate, and no one dares tell the truth for fear of the lord's displeasure with those who tell the truth, for the lord does not want to hear evil spoken of his men. And there is a common saying around the court: My lord has very good manners since he refuses to hear those who speak evil of his people. Alas, 'good manners' ought to include the desire to hear the truth! But if anyone is accused falsely through envy, as can happen, when the lord has inquired into the truth, he ought to punish and dismiss the accuser as an envious liar; in this way his people will fear to do evil and will cease the evils they have done. But these things the good prince should not allow.

He ought to desire that his subjects perform their best in whatever office God has placed them. The nobles ought to do what they ought to do, the clerics attend to their studies, and to the divine service, the merchants to their merchandise, the artisans to their craft, the laborers to the cultivation of the earth, and thus each one whatever his rank, ought to live by good policy, without extortion nor over-charging, so that each may live properly under him, and that they love him as a good prince ought to be loved by his people, and that he have from them the legal revenue that is reasonable to collect and take from his country, without gnawing to the bone his poor commoners. When asked why he did not collect larger taxes from his people, the Emperor Tiberias* responded, Valerius tells us, "the good shepherd shears his sheep only once a year; he does not fleece them all the time, nor skin them so that he draws blood."

## Chapter 11 The love that the prince ought to have for his subjects

Now let us examine a little the rights of the prince according to the law; that is, whether the good prince can raise any new taxes or subsidies above his usual revenue over his demesne for any reason. It seems to me that the laws give enough freedom and permit him to do so for some cause. For example, to defend the land from his enemies if he is attacked by war, for which he ought to have paid soldiers for the defense of the country. Also for marrying his children, or for paying ransom* for them if they should be captured. And in this case especially, the good prince can raise a new tax over and above his natural demesne over his subjects without infringing on the law.

But this should be done compassionately and discretely so to hinder the poor less, and without taking more than what is necessary for the particular cause, such as war or for whatever it was set. And the rich, in this case, ought to support the poor, and not exempt the rich, as is done nowadays, leaving the poor the more heavily burdened. I dare say, no matter who is displeased, saving their reverence, it is a marvelous right that the rich and high officials of the king or princes who have their rank and power as a gift of the king and princes and are able to carry the burden, are exempt from taxes, and the poor who have nothing from the king have to pay. Is it not reasonable if I have given a great gift to my servant, and give him a rich livelihood and his estate, and it happened that I had some need, that he comes to my aid more than the one who has had nothing from me? It is a strange custom that is used nowadays in this kingdom in the setting of taxes. But if it were changed, it must be uniform, not that some of the rich pay and others not, for this would bring envy, because some would despise those who paid as a form of servitude.* If everyone paid, no one would be reproached. Nevertheless I do not mean that those who fought for the defense of the country should not be exempt. I say these things for the poor. Compassion moves me because their tears and moans come bitterly forth. There are some who come to pay this money imposed on them and then they and their poor household starve afterwards, and sell their beds and other poor possessions cheaply and for nothing. And it would please God if someone informed the king and noble princes. There is no doubt that their noble blood holds so much kindness that they could not allow such cruelty. But often those that collect these payments are fat and rich, and so whether all this comes to the profit of the project for which the tax was established, God knows, and so do others! Without doubt, taxes like these are used for superfluities or for any other reason than pure necessity, it is sinful for those who established it, and a very grave burden.

The noble Romans were pagans and unbelievers, yet were so well governed that we ought to take them for an example. As Valerius says, it was the law of Rome that all manner of goods gathered for war could only be for this use, and no other. Because superfluity of wine and meat, taken superfluously, causes one to require more rest, thus, the body desires rest more than the hard work of fighting or thinking. If I were allowed to say something more about this how much more could I say; but the knowledge of these things does not please the evil ministers who have enriched themselves, and they will reprimand me. I could tell them without arrogance something that Euripides,* the great poet, said to the Athenians who asked him to quote a sentence from a tragedy that he had written. "Tragedy," said Valerius, "is a way of writing that represents misdeeds done on the orders of the polity; either by the community, or by princes." He said that he did not write his sayings in order to reprimand nor to be reprimanded, but in order to teach us to live well. About the poet, Valerius said that he would not dishonor himself by obeying the words of the people and ignoring his own. Valerius also said on this that it is certain that fealty is admirable when born of and come from reason, and also that he who has great reason can judge the truth of his own work. He has just cause to uphold it when it is not out of pride nor arrogance, but to uphold the merit of the thing which he feels is noble and glorious in itself. For, he says, whoever praises someone for his virtue desires to be praised for the same thing, for both of them come from the same spirit and wisdom.

## Chapter 12 Examples from ancient deeds of the above ideas

To conclude what was said before, that is, the good prince desires his people's welfare more than his own, and he should not set much store by the riches gathered for him, nor in anything for his private benefit, let us look at the Romans again as an example. These are Valerius' own words: Worthy Roman princes, he says, had taken to heart the love of the public good, and set so little by their own benefit that their daughters had to be married at the expense of the community, since they had so little money saved that they could not marry them as their high honor required. And when the greatest of them had passed away (the very good Fabricius,* also Scipio Africanus,* who were such worthy men, other dignified conquerors, and great and noble princes of Rome), their debts and their funeral expenses were paid from the common treasury, which the people consented to willingly, in contemplation of the merit of the great good that these nobles had done. They had nothing but their great and steadfast good deeds. Because despite the fact that in fortune's goods they were poor, nevertheless they were rich in the great and noble honors that they deserved and merited, from which it appears and is true, that the most worthy are not always the most rich, nor most fortunate as to wealth.

But fortune aids them in another more admirable manner when she helps them acquire the highest fame and honors. For despite the poverty of these brave conquerors and noble men, they were dictators or consuls, that is, as we would say, emperors or the highest sovereign princes. And many times they celebrated their victory with a triumph, which was a marvelous honor that the Romans gave their princes and rulers when they had great victories, as we will describe below. For in Rome great virtues were their riches and the spirit of men and women was very vigorous then. The more virtuous one was, the more dignity he had, because one was not concerned with how much he had, but how much he was worth in goodness and wisdom. Those who had the most virtue were highest in authority, about which Valerius said these beautiful words: Such things reconcile lords and join them as equals; such things have power within and without; for by this law everyone's intent was the good of the country and not his own, saying that princes would rather be poor in a rich empire, than to be rich and have plenty in a poor country. So they were given recompense so that these noble men were saved from suffering by the wealth of the republic.

And since we are on the subject of these noble Roman princes, since their noble virtues ought to be an example and a mirror to every good prince and worthy man, let us tell more of them.

Valerius tells of another worthy consul named Marcus Turnius who was a very great conqueror and won many lordships for the Romans. When once there was a siege before the city of Samite, the spies of the Samites reported that he was in poor shape at the siege, with soldiers enough but insufficient supplies and food. Then the citizens sent messengers to him with great gifts, believing that they could bribe him. His response to them was written down by Valerius to show his constancy and bravery. He said that Marcus Turnius (who was a clear and well polished mirror of the holy rule of temperance and virtue), wanted the messengers to see on what food he dined and what his situation was. So seated on a bench before the fire, he was served a small portion of food on wooden dishes.

Nonetheless, he refused their gifts, great presents of gold and silver, and rich vessels, and answered them, saying that he would rather be master of his wealth, than have his wealth master him, because it seemed to him that he was master in so far as he could despise or refuse it. But if he had taken it, it would have conquered him. "And you remember," he said, "that Marcus will not be conquered by gifts nor captured in battle."

This Marcus Turnius was so great a man that he defeated King Pyrrhus* who had come to the aid of the city of Tarento against the Romans. In his army, Pyrrhus had 80,000 foot soldiers and 120,000 on horseback, of which 30,000 were killed and 13,000 taken prisoner. Pyrrhus himself fled into Italy in the fifth year of war. It was a very great victory for the Romans, but the good prince would never enrich himself but wanted everything distributed to the horsemen and men at arms, except for what he sent to the treasury in Rome. For himself, he retained only the honor, and that was sufficient for him; he wanted others to have the revenue.

Another story of great virtue from Valerius: Among the other princes of Rome was a worthy man, a consul named Fabricius, whom I have already mentioned, who seemed to be of such great virtue that despite his lack of wealth, he refused great and notable gifts which King Pyrrhus sent him believing that he could bribe him. This Fabricius had such a reputation for nobility and loyalty that King Pyrrhus his adversary said of him that the sun would lose its radiance before Fabricius lost his loyalty. King Pyrrhus' doctor came to Fabricius saying that he would poison his master if he would pay him well, but the very worthy man answered that this means to victory was not used by the Romans. So he took the doctor and sent him back to Pyrrhus, for which kindness and by virtue of his loyalty, he liked him so well that he offered for love of him to make peace with the Romans, and not trouble them any more if they would allow him to keep in peace the lands he had already conquered. But the valiant man would not accept such a peace, but only if Pyrrhus would leave behind all that he had won from the Romans and their land. Then Pyrrhus used all his power to bring Fabricius over to his side. And when he saw that he could not, he praised his virtue so much that he said that he would never again fight him in the field, and although they were ready for battle, he took himself back to Tarento.

Valerius tells more of this Fabricius: it was recounted in his presence that there was a philosopher in Athens who followed a sect and way of life which taught that humans should do nothing except for delight and bodily ease.* This worthy man greatly despised these ideas and words, he believed them vain, foolish, and dishonorable, and that all pleasure, not only of the body but of the soul as well, if not earned in virtue ought to be despised. But for those that are good, delight in doing well is their reward. And this saying is true, says Valerius, and appears certain. Because the city of Athens which was governed by great labor and the study of wisdom and virtue was conquered by pleasures and lust, losing its supremacy. The city of Rome, as long as it was obsessed by the exercise of virtue, conquered, won and overcame all other rulers, and how Athens lost its virtue will be told below.

And still on the subject of the good prince loving the public good of his country, a king named Epaminondas* was a prince of marvelous virtue and held his enemies subject to him. He was brought down in battle by a lance through his body, and as he was dying he had such joy that he had overcome his enemies that he did not grieve at his death. So he said these words to those around him: "now the gods have given me the happiness to see my city of Thebes the chief city of Greece, and the great and courageous city of Lacedemonia* is brought down by us and made subject to us. I do not die without heirs, for I leave you these two daughters that I have begotten," (he meant these two cities, because he had no heirs of his body). He understood that he would live in memory because of these two cities he had conquered, just as children remember their fathers.

Justin praised this Epaminondas who captured many kingdoms, not for himself, but for his country, but because he had so little greed, after his death they did not find enough to cover his funeral. He was no more profligate than he was greedy, but carried his rank so temperately that his virtue was apparent. The reason with which he lived his life was not lost on his deathbed, as Valerius reveals. And when he was brought half-dead back to his lodgings, when he had recovered his spirit a bit, he asked those around him whether his shield had been captured from him after he fell. When he heard that it had not, he was filled with joy, had it brought to him, and kissed it, and asked about the victory.

When he was told, he said "then all is well" and died. After his death, the Athenians, who were often tested in battle by his virtue and strength, became lazy and idle, busying themselves with vain things, which caused their downfall.

## Chapter 13 The reason why Valerius is so often quoted in this book

Because of the noble book which the great Valerius wrote about the deeds of the Romans, I quote him more than any other. He has given me the subject on which to speak and to prove by example the pure intention that I have, which is, as I said before, to give reason to inspire courage in virtue and in living well, for princes, for knights and nobles, and also for the common people. For, as that same Valerius says, examples of virtue move one more than simple words to desire honor and courage more and to love of virtue, as Aristotle attests in the tenth book of *Ethics*: therefore, in following the style of the noble author Valerius in order to increase courage in those who desire this doctrine of virtuous works, by which one acquires true honor, I am moved to show diverse examples of things that happened to many magnificent men in the past, who for their merit are memorialized in this book. To hear about them gives great pleasure, desire and hope for honors to noble spirits, for honors make us desire virtue. For we see that honor is given for all serious and excellent things, such as great courage or great knowledge or other virtue. For this is why I call these worthy brave Roman conquerors "princes", because they seem like them even if they have neither rule, or extensive lands, nor riches. But according to the fashion of Valerius, Romans attributed the greatness of men to courage and virtue and not to wealth, and thus he calls them not only princes, but in his book calls them "emperors" in several chapters, men such as Scipio Africanus, Pompey* the Great, Sulla and others, even though they were never vested with empire.

## Chapter 14 On liberality in princes and examples of the Romans

We will continue our subject of the second of the three things that are necessary to the good prince, which is that he love the public good.

The good prince who loves the universal good more than his own should be liberal, a very necessary quality from which he will profit triply; first it is for the good of his soul (if he is discreet), secondly, for the praise and honor of his reputation; thirdly, he will attract the hearts of his own subjects to himself as well as those of strangers. There is no doubt that nothing profits a prince as much as discreet generosity. Oh, how much the Romans profited from it! Once when the ambassadors of Carthage came to Rome to ransom the prisoners who had been taken in battle during the wars between them, the Romans returned freely, without ransom, 1,747 noble young men, who were rich and of high rank. Valerius exalts and praises this three-fold generosity in three ways. "O what marvelous generosity, to free such a great force of the enemy, to deprive themselves of such a ransom, to pardon such injuries." "I believe," he said, "that the ambassadors marvelled at such generosity." Then he added, "Oh Roman magnificence, equal to the kindness of gods, for this gesture was more generous than your enemies could dare ask." There is no doubt that because of their liberality, the Romans acquired sovereignty and dominion more than by force, because foreign countries seeing their noble and free customs, yielded to them, not in hopes of being servants, but in order to be free. And Valerius said the same, that the empire of Rome, that is, its superiority, did not increase so much from the strength of their bodies as from the vigor of their courage. Valerius tells us (which I have quoted from his book word-for-word because of its beauty and substance) that he could give generosity no better company than humanity and mercy, for they deserve all kinds of praise. And he says that generosity shows itself to those who are poor and suffering, who need one to be generous and liberal to them. Humanity is shown to those who are ill or in prison or insecure in their bodies or their goods. He who has power and right to punish and to pardon, pardons and alleviates their miseries by the power of the prince. He is responsible for healing them his poor subjects compassionately, by the above virtues, maintaining the order of justice and not too rigorously, and especially in those things that are not contrary to nature. And even though, said Valerius, you do not know which of the virtues to praise most, nonetheless, it seems that the one that is highest is that which takes its name from God, and this means liberality which is so like divine virtue, extending itself to all and by which one acquires the most friends. And as it is more in the power of princes than in other persons to be liberal and also they are most in need of friends and well wishers, I say that it is most necessary and appropriate and even enhances their glory. It is written in the third book, thirteenth chapter of the *Policraticus*, that Titus* the Emperor by his liberality atoned for the vice of avarice which had been his father's, in such a manner that he was called by all the darling and delight of the human race. And Tully,* in book 2 of *On Duties*, said that there is no worse vice in a prince or in those who govern the republic than avarice.

But since we say so often that the good prince ought to be generous, it is important to say in what manner on and what things he should extend his liberality. So Seneca declares in the second book of *On Benefices*, that the prince or the giver must understand his own power and authority, and also the power and rank of him to whom he would give, so as not to give a lesser gift than is appropriate, nor to give more than appropriate. The prince or the donor ought to consider to whom and why he gives the gift, because there is a difference between giving for merit, as a reward for something well done, and giving out of the frank generosity of pure courtesy.

Because, if merited, the prince ought to look closely that the gift be such that it can not be blamed as shabby or cheap. It ought always to be as generous as is merited. But when the gift is given without great desert or merit, although it is the role of a prince or powerful person to give as great a gift as appropriate, nonetheless they can also give small ones to poor and indigent persons. This liberality must also be moderate and tempered by discretion, as Tully says in the book quoted above. For let us suppose that the prince or another gives willingly and generously from his wealth, he still ought to consider how he will continue in that virtue and not be like those who give foolishly and distribute without any order. This generosity ought to be from his own wealth and not that of some other person. As St. Ambrose said in the first book of *On Duties*, it is not "liberality" when one gives to one and takes from others, because nothing is generous if it is not just. This is why generosity is the divine virtue in the good prince. And it is always appropriate for the prince to reward the friendship which others give him, and not in this case to apportion the gift to the weakness of the persons who did him service, but to the grandeur of the recipient, who can reward well. As is written of King Darius [I]* of Persia (Not that Darius [III]* that fought against Alexander but the one who became ruler by trickery when he made his horse neigh, when they could not agree on which of them should be heir to the king and tend the kingdom: the princes had made a law that they would gather before the temple in the morning and whoever's horse neighed first would be king. The night before, Darius brought his horse to a mare at the meeting place, and because of this when his horse smelled the scent of the mare the next morning, his horse neighed first. So he became king of Persia.) This Darius was not yet wealthy. A man named Philomites out of his goodness and without being asked, gave him a cloak which pleased Darius greatly. When Darius came to be king, he did not forget this courtesy and gave him the city and the whole island of Samos, which is a good island, where Pythagoras* the philosopher was born. Thus Darius did not consider the price of the gift, but rather the generosity of the giver, and the power of the person giving the reward.

Also, Mithridates, the wealthy king who ruled twenty-two countries, showed his great generosity by rewarding one of his knights, who was named Leonicus by getting him out of the prison of his enemies, for he had been captured in battle. He turned over a very large number of prisoners [in exchange], because he preferred to increase the number of his enemies than leave unrewarded someone who well deserved it.

## Chapter 15 On the humane pity of the prince

We have spoken enough of the liberality of the good prince. Now we ought to speak of the other two virtues which accompany the first in merit and praise; that is humanity and clemency. These are necessary to have in a good prince, and to prove this we will use examples.

There was the humanity that the worthy Roman prince Lucius Emilius Paulus* showed to King Perses* who was defeated in a battle so completely that Perses was taken prisoner. But when he knew who stood before him, the noble man would not allow Perses to kneel before him. He took him kindly by the hand and brought him with him, comforted him and honored him, made him sit at table and in council with him, despite Perses' hesitation, and thus treated him as gently as a brother. Ah, what a noble virtue in a prince and in all captains and soldiers, to have pity and be humane to those they have conquered!

There is the example of Hector* of Troy of whom one reads that no lion was more fierce or cruel than he was in battle. But when his enemies came before him humiliated and crying for mercy, then no lamb could be more gentle nor more good natured than he was, and so he treated them most gently, as his brothers, by which he profited as much, for his great good nature brought many to surrender to him. So every noble brave prince and good man ought to act thus, and not do as many lords and soldiers do today. When they conquer lands, fortresses, cities, or other places, they act like famished dogs when they enter the city, without pity for the horrible massacres they inflict on Christians – dishonoring women and leaving everything in ruin. Alas, what hearts these men have, when such cruelty can be done to others in their likeness, which is against nature and against divine law! Are they not afraid that the fierce devils of Hell will snatch them for the city of Hell? For there is no doubt that they will come to that at the end. And certainly such people ought rather to have the face and flesh of a horrible serpent, rather than human ones, for under the human form, they wear the cruelty of the treasonable detestable beast!

Marcus Marcellus,* who was one of the princes of Rome with great authority, did not do this. When by his great valor, he captured the strong and noble city of Syracuse, he went up to the highest castle to survey the fortune of the city, and considered the power which was maintained, by such noble kings, and the power it had on land and sea. It was then filled with sorrow and so brought down that he had pity on his enemy, and he started to weep.

Yet there are those who are so cruel and inhumane towards their prisoners that because of greed they force them to pay a larger ransom than they can. It is horrible to hear and see the varied tortures that many do to their prisoners, so cruel and horrible that the Saracens could do no worse! And if such torturers die a good death it seems to me that God and nature do them a great wrong, but I do not doubt that they are punished, for God is just.

Ah, the very excellent Prince Pompey never did such, he who was so superior in excellence of arms that he conquered every part of the Orient with his sword. But when he had subjugated King Tigranes* of Armenia, among others, and killed 40,000 of his men, and had him brought before him, Tigranes took his crown off and placed it at the feet of Pompey, and weeping thought to kneel down before him. But Pompey would not allow him to. Then he very gently raised him up, put his crown back on his head, comforted him, and reestablished him in his rank under obedience to the Romans. It seemed to him that it was as great an honor to make a king as to defeat one.

## Chapter 16 On the clemency and good nature which the prince must have

We have spoken of the humanity of the good prince. Now we will speak of the virtue of clemency which he ought especially to have towards his subjects in order to tie their hearts to him and confirm them in greatest affection. For without doubt there is nothing more sweet nor more favorable to a subject than to see his lord and prince gentle and kind to him, and nothing can satisfy the hearts of his men and his familiars more than mercy, gentleness and kindness do, when wisely and discreetly done. Not that he abases himself among them so that they respect him less, but while keeping the honor which a sovereign deserves to receive from his subjects, he is gentle and kind with their requests and petitions, and of gentle speech. He should not show great annoyance or disdain towards any of them for some small thing or misdeed, because the higher and stronger foundation a tower has, the less it will take the shock of a little stone.

Philocrates,* the king or duke of Athens, had great good nature. He had a friend named Transippus. Sitting at supper together, in the heat of anger he said many injurious and hateful things to Philocrates. But he did not lose his temper nor say anything to injure him, but he begged him not to be angry nor to go away angry from supper. Transippus, compelled by his anger, then spat in his face, but despite this he did not become angry. Then he sent his sons out, because they wanted passionately to kill him and avenge the majesty of their father. The next day Philocrates knew that Transippius was overcome with shame and anger with himself for what he had done and said, and he wanted to kill himself, and Philocrates was moved to great pity. He went immediately to him, embraced him and comforted him, and pardoned him gently, and he gave his word that he was and would be in his grace as before.

Yet more on the good nature of this prince Philocrates. He had a most beautiful young daughter. A young man loved her so much that he thought he would die. Once, he saw her walking with her mother down the street. The young man was so struck by love that he could not control himself and kissed her in front of everyone when he passed her. The mother of the girl, Philocrates' wife, wanted the young man to be executed for this and strongly insisted on this to her lord. But Philocrates answered, compassionately "if we kill those that love us, what could we do to those that hate us?" This response was most humane.

Also Pompey, the brave man spoken of before, is described as having such great courage that he was not lightly moved. He patiently endured many injuries from the envious, for he was very careful to preserve and increase the public good. But despite them, he never let up, from which it appears to be true, as Valerius said in the first chapter of the third book of *On Patience*; patience is so like strength that it is born of it and with it.

Should we not give another little example of good nature of the very chivalrous prince and king, Pyrrhus of whom we have spoken already many times? He had very great courage and many virtues. He honored the good and valiant as he often showed the Romans during the wars between them. Once in battle he defeated the Romans, but however, he was not arrogant to them like nowadays, when some are proud of a lucky victory (which is a great folly, because one ought to remember that fortune is distributed as she wills, and often gives such victories and then the next time, the wheel turns and luck changes). But this Pyrrhus, who knew how brave the Romans were, despite his victory, when their ambassadors came, he knew they came to reclaim their prisoners, and he received and honored them greatly and sent his knights there to honor them.

## Chapter 17 Yet again on good nature and how fortune may change

Still on the subject of the wise kindness of the prince and also how fortune can turn in a minute, we have the example of what happened to that same King Pyrrhus, by which we can conclude that it is true that a man does not owe his good fortune to pride. King Pyrrhus was a great warrior and victorious over many princes and kings, but

just as fortune aided him sometimes to acquire kingdoms and lordships, it seemed to deny them to him also, often bringing him to lose
them by tragic defeats and, finally brought him to his last end in
battle. So since he waged war in many countries, the land of Greece
was very much afraid of him, because of the battles that he had
fought against the Romans and the Carthaginians. He attacked a city
of Greece called Lacedemonia which was once very famous. But this
time it was better defended by the women than the men from being
destroyed by force; so says Valerius. In order to defend the city and
the country, such a large number of women fought that it forced
Pyrrhus into shameful retreat, and one of his sons was killed there,
which weighed heavily on him. So, he did not find fortune prosper-
ous. When he left, he went to the city of Arges and was killed by a
hurled stone. So, King Pyrrhus, who had tormented many on earth,
met his own end.

Helenus, the son of Antigonus King of Arges, was very happy at
the death of Pyrrhus, and severed the head from his body carried it
to his father, and with great joy. But Antigonus a very wise prince,
scolded him for forgetting misfortune and the fragility of human
events, in taking such joy at the ruin of so great a man. He honored
the head and took off his own head covering, that of the kings of
Macedonia, and honored and covered the head of Pyrrhus. And so
he had head and body reverently brought to the field with honorable
funeral rites according to their custom. And he had the son of
Pyrrhus, who had been brought to him as a prisoner, dressed in royal
robes, told him to take on the courage of a king, gave him the ashes
of his father's body in a golden vessel, and let him go back to Epirus,
his country. And it truly seems to me, that this story shows not only
the mutability of fortune, but also the act of a generous, humane and
merciful prince, as reflected in the deed of Antigonus.

Like him, it is written that Hannibal,* Emperor of Africa, was a
worthy knight and fought many victorious battles against the Romans,
and also sometimes lost. When he had victory in any battle he had
the battlefield searched and any high ranking princes and knights
that were found dead, even among his enemies he would have taken
up and buried very honorably, just as he did for the brave Roman
prince Emilius Paulus* who was killed in the battle of Cannae.*
There was so great a slaughter of Romans that Hannibal, who had
the battle field searched, sent to his country three barrels of gold

rings, taken from the fingers of slain noblemen (to wear rings was the custom of nobles then). And if this story seems marvelous and hard to believe, there is the testimony of all the historians who have spoken of it. (But perhaps the barrel was not as large as they are today in France, but was another measure given the same name.)

He not only had the body of this Emilius honorably brought in, but also that of another Roman prince named Tiberius Graccus who was killed in another battle, and sent his ashes to his knights in a vessel of gold to be carried to his country. He did the same for Marcus Marcellus who was killed in another battle, had his body dressed honorably and the head crowned with laurel as the victor, for he had won the battle against Hannibal, despite his being killed. Thus was the nobility of spirit of this prince Hannibal who honored his enemies when he defeated them as well as he would be honored had he been victor, for which Valerius said that his humanity earned greater fame and praise for Hannibal than his victories did, for his victories came from the cleverness of Africa, but his praise from the courtesy and kindness of Rome.

## Chapter 18 How the good prince ought not be proud of any good fortune

Since we have already discussed that a person should not be proud of good fortune, which can change, in order to keep the good prince from such arrogance, let us give more examples. For, says Valerius, the Romans were conquerors because they were not proud of their good fortune at all, as some are who are crazy with joy when prosperity comes to them. But the Romans said they gained more by sparing the vanquished, that is by letting them go mercifully, than by conquering.

What is true is that often good fortune blinds people by burdening them with such great pride that they do not know themselves and do not understand the game she is playing. And then they are thrown into a dark pit of despair, as appears in the example of Hannibal, the prince of Carthage mentioned above. Despite his many beautiful virtues, he became so proud of his victory over the Romans in the battle of Cannae where so many noble Romans had died (as was told before), that he no longer deigned to hear those who wanted to speak to him but would only speak through others who reported to him.

He trusted so much in his good sense, good fortune and happiness that it seemed to him that no one could teach him anything. Because of this, he distrusted the words of a wise knight named Maharbal, who had understood and showed Hannibal by what means he could capture Rome in only a few days and dine in the Capitol (which was the chief fortress of the city). But he disdained to hear him because he believed that he was his own best advisor and that he had so much sense that he could not fail. But his thoughts deceived him and he did fail. Because of this, no prince should despise hearing many different opinions especially from wise persons. For there is nothing, no matter how subtle, that the human imagination can not find and attain. But the proud will not deign to inquire, for as Valerius says, "happiness according to the common course will not allow a proud man to hear the voice of the humble even if it is truthful or profitable to him, because he is neither moderate nor temperate."

Hannibal's end was described in the *History of the Romans*. After a long time of fighting against the Romans in many battles, fortune turned so much against him that he finally lost all his empire, his people, and his goods, and he was forced to flee in retreat. But he could find no prince in the world who would welcome him, because they were afraid of the Romans. This brought him to despair and he killed himself by drinking venom. And thus, Hannibal, who had been in his time one of the most chivalrous princes and most fortunate in the world, according to the stories, died miserably. On our subject, Solon,* who was one of the seven sages, said that contrary to those who think they can find happiness and felicity in this world by riches, honors, and pleasures, one must never believe a person to be happy who lives in this world, because, until our last day we are subject to fortune who is untrustworthy and changeable, and change takes the name "happy" away from human creatures.

## Chapter 19 How the good prince ought to love justice

According to my judgment, we have sufficiently discussed the subject of the first two points and the branches that descend from them, on how the natural and non-tyrannical good prince ought to establish and build his government, as we promised before. First he ought to love and fear God above all else. Secondly, he loves and cares for the public good of his land and country more than his own good. Now it remains to speak of the third point, which is that he ought to keep and maintain justice. It is appropriate to speak first on what justice is. Afterwards, how to keep it is necessary, and how the ancients were well trained to keep it. We will use appropriate examples of these things as we did previously.

"Justice," said Aristotle, "is a measure which renders to each his due," and much more could be said in describing this virtue. But on this subject I have spoken elsewhere, especially in the *Book of Human Wisdom*, so I will discuss this the more briefly at present so as to present some examples. The good prince ought to keep justice in such fashion that no favoritism will lead him to impede or to destroy it. Our ancestors loved justice so much that they did not spare even their own children. There was once an emperor who proclaimed an edict that anyone who broke a certain law would lose his two eyes. When it was broken by his own son, rather than blind his own heir so that he could not govern the republic, he found a remedy to satisfy the punishment without preventing the son from governing one day. But this remedy was too pitiful: his son had one of his eyes put out, and he put out his own, as the other. I say that justice was kept more rigorously than it is now.

And on evil ministers I have spoken of before, so I will not discuss them here. On the subject of the great rigor of justice, the noble Roman prince named Aulus Postumus did not do less. He defeated a group of people called the Volscii* through his sense, great boldness, and bravery. But before the battle began he had announced that, under pain of death, no one was to be so bold that he could begin to fight or even go out of his lodgings without permission. Then Aulus Postumus went for a little while away from his army for some business that he had. He had a son who knew where a great number of the enemy were hiding, so he rushed out with a force of men, fought, and defeated them. When his father came back and discovered this, he judged that the greater evil would be to save from death one who had broken the law of the prince, and as an example, despite the victory over the enemies, he had his son's head cut off.

But to pass from examples of great rigor, let us discuss how the good prince keeps justice and what is necessary for him to do so. First, and principally, to do this he ought to be provided with wise and prudent men and good councillors, who love his soul and honor and the good of the country more than their own benefit. But I fear that presently there are not very many! If the prince has wise councillors he can maintain the rule of justice and other particular laws, and increase and multiply the virtue, strength, power and wealth of his country. Oh, who is the prince who can sufficiently deserve the wise, loyal, and good counsellor because of the great good that comes from following his advice if he wants to believe him? Is it not said in the *History of the Romans* that the wise Scipio Nasica* (who was of the lineage of the other noble Scipios who were so valiant in warfare) despite the fact that he did not live by his weapons like the others, he was so wise and prudent in the council and governing of the republic that he did as much by his wisdom as the others did by their weapons?

Using his lively intelligence he fought against some of the powerful Romans who wanted to overpower the Senate and the good of the people. Valerius said about him that he deserved no less praise in his "coat of peace" than other warriors deserved in their "coat of arms" because he defended the city from many great problems and much good resulted because of him.

## Chapter 20 What councillors the prince ought to have

Now it is appropriate to consider what people the prince should choose as his councillors. Should he choose from among the young? No, because they counselled Jeroboam badly in the past as they have many others. Therefore they should be chosen from the old, the most wise and experienced, because they are more capable and ready to advise than the young. It is necessary that the loyal councillor be well-informed on the things about which he counsels. He should not believe lightly in a thing that appears good before proving its truth, examining and inquiring. At first glance a thing may appear to be what it is not. In the *Rhetoric*, Aristotle said that the old and elderly did not have the habit of believing lightly, because they had been defrauded in their lives many times. They do not make decisions on doubtful things, but often interpret things for the worst, because many times they have seen the worst happen, thus they will not give advice hastily. They do not put great hopes on a little foundation and little evidence, because many times they have seen things come to pass differently from how one thought they would, and so they will not advise great undertakings without serious consideration. Most commonly these things are the opposite in the young, as other habits are naturally more weighty in the old. But I do not say that all the old are wise! For Aristotle says that there are two kinds of age; one which follows after a well-ordered and temperate youth, which Tully [Cicero] praises in his book *On Old Age*. The other is age which comes after a wasted and dissolute youth, and it is subject to many miseries and is not worth recommending. Thus I have said that the prince ought to choose councillors from the old and the wise. To speak more of them; although they do not have great bodily strength, like the young, all the same, they are greater in virtue and discreet in advice, which is more useful and more profitable than bodily strength, and is so much more to be praised. And the most noble virtues are understanding, discretion, and knowledge rather than strength of body. Where the wisdom and counsel of the old and wise are followed, the royal majesties, cities, politics, and public affairs are well governed and sustained, which are often destroyed by the young, as Tully says, and which appears clear in many histories. Thus while age takes away bodily strength it abounds in strength of intelligence and understanding, which are more praiseworthy things. And as for those who in age regret youth, it is a sign that they are neither virtuous nor wise, because he is not wise who has not chosen the more profitable thing. Some disparage age because they are deprived of the bodily pleasures and delights. But, age is not to be blamed but greatly praised therefore, for it uproots the root of all evils. According to Archica of Tarento, who was a great philosopher, no more greater pestilence was given to humans by nature than bodily desire, which gives birth to treachery, subversion of cities and of peoples, rapes, and all evils. There is no evil that sensuality will not attract the human spirit to do. It is that which extinguishes the judgment of reason and blinds the human soul, and it has no affinity nor connection with virtue. Thus, one does better to praise and choose old age which has intellectual delights more commonly than youth does, which are more noble, and do not lead to misfortune and contradiction; as Aristotle says in the eighth book of the *Ethics*. As Tully says, old age is stronger and more courageous than youth. Solon, the Sage of Athens, said to the tyrant Pisistratus,* when he asked him why he spoke to him so boldly and confidently, [Solon] answered, that it was the strength of age. And this is told in the work by Valerius, from which I have plucked a few good tales on my subject of justice in order to describe what advisors a good prince should have.

## Chapter 21 How a good prince, despite being good natured and kind, ought to be feared

The nature of justice and what it serves and to what extent is well known and understood; it is appropriate for the good prince to punish (or have punished) evildoers. And so I will pass by this for a time and proceed to that which also befits the good prince: The virtue of justice, which renders to each that which is his due, according to his power. If he keeps this rule, which is just, he will not fail to do equity in everything, and thus, he will render to himself his due. For it is rational that he has the same right he gives to everyone, which means that he would be obeyed and feared by right and by reason, as is appropriate to the majesty of a prince.

For in whatever land or place where a prince is not feared, there is no true justice. How it is appropriate for the prince to be feared is shown by the worthy man Clearcus who was Duke of Lacedemonia (which is a large part of Greece where there once was a marvelously valiant people). This duke was so chivalrous and great a warrior that his people were more afraid to flee than to die. He told them that soldiers should be more afraid of their prince than death and their enemies. Because of his words and also the punishment that he gave malefactors and cowards, they gave themselves without sparing, by which they achieved marvelous things. There is no doubt that the good prince ought to be feared despite being gentle and benign. His kindness ought to be considered a thing of grace which one ought to particularly heed rather than scorn. It is for this reason the ancients painted the goddess of lordship as a seated lady of very high rank on a royal throne, holding in one hand an olive branch and in the other a naked sword, showing that rule must include kindness and mercy as well as justice and power.

The good prince, as was said before, is governed by old sages and gives to everyone his due, as is in his power. And he prefers that these good and meritorious persons, are honored for their virtues, according to the wise saying: "Rise in the presence of the bald man." In times past, the old and wise were honored most, especially by the

Lacedemonians who were honorable Greeks. This began with the introduction of the laws of Lycurgus, the noble and brave king who governed them. Then they had beautiful customs and maintained them a long time. Once upon a time, a very old man went to the theater in Athens to see the games. The theater was a place for the young men to wrestle each other, if armed, in jousts or battles, or in other ways, but none of the citizens of Athens would give up a place for this old man to sit down, so he went around to the place where the legates, which we call ambassadors, of Lacedemonia sat, who had come with a message to Athens. According to their custom those who were young honored the old, and they all stood up and set him in a honorable place among them. And when the people [of Athens] saw this they greatly approved of the noble custom of this foreign city, and said among themselves, "we know well what is right, but we should pay attention to the foreigners."

## Chapter 22 How the good prince ought to use the good counsel of the wise

We have said how the good prince honors the wise. Now we will describe how he follows their advice. A knight, captain called Municius, as Valerius recounts, wanted to give thanks to Fabius, by whom he and his army were saved. "Fair lords," he said to his knights, "I have often heard say that he is first in action who knows how to give good advice, and he is second who follows good advice, but the one who neither acknowledges advice nor follows it is useless. And because of this, fair lords," he said, "nature removes from us the first, that is, we are not wise enough to give advice, because we have not lively intelligence enough. Therefore let us do the second, that is, obey Fabius who is wise and gives good counsel." And so they did, and because of his wisdom, they were victorious in battle.

And on the subject of believing the wise and following their advice, [Aristotle's] great *Dialectic* says that one ought to believe each expert in his art. This means that the good prince ought to consult a variety of people according to the variety of things to do. For the governance of justice and the diverse important cases which he hears, he ought not to take advice from his soldiers nor his knights, but from jurists and clerks of this science. The same with warfare; not from clerks but from knights, and similarly in other matters. As Valerius said

about Quintus Scaevola, despite his being a very wise jurist and inter-
preter of the law, every time someone came to him to ask advice on
any custom of the offices of Rome, he sent those who asked to Furius
or to Castellanus, who were experts on these customs, even if by
chance he knew them just as well. But he wanted everyone to take
care of the branch of knowledge to which one was devoted, no more.
By which fact, said Valerius, he confirmed his authority, more
because he did not claim for himself any office, than because of the
superiority of his own knowledge. This is unlike those who out of
envy of others and arrogance want to meddle in everything.

The good prince should follow the advice of the wise in order to
do justice and equity to himself and to others, ensure that those he
has commissioned to office are not corrupted nor of evil life, and he
should see to it that his judges do not favor one party more than
another, as was discussed before, and ensure that the powerful are
not spared more than the humble. Yet commonly the rich are favored
over the poor, which is against God, against right, and against reason.
Anacharsis* the philosopher compared law to spider webs, and said
that the spider webs never caught fat flies nor wasps, but catch little
flies and frail butterflies, while letting strong birds go, which often
destroy them when they fly through. So it is with the law, because
the great and powerful often break it and pass through without fear,
but the little flies are caught and trapped. This commonly happens
to the poor and humble people because of the avarice of ministers
of justice. And on this Pericles* (who was a wise man and of great
authority in the city of Athens, and the most virtuous as Tully tells
us in his *On Duties*), said that whoever administers justice should
have not only have continent hands and tongue but also his eyes,
which means that a judge ought to keep from receiving gifts which
corrupt human judgment. Also he should keep himself both from
talking too much and from incontinence of the flesh, for the common
people take the life of judges and of the powerful as an example.

## Chapter 23 How the good prince ought to observe the actions of his officers

Because we have begun the subject of how the good prince ought to
be careful to take heed of the actions of his officers; if not, it can be
most prejudicial to the kingdom or ruler in that most often princes

are blamed for the bad deeds of their ministers and officers, without the ruler knowing anything about it. Let us discuss this subject at a bit more length, as it will be expedient to give examples. Because commonly today persons are put in royal office, and in power as judges, or governing others – usually through favor or the help of friends – one scarcely questions their virtues and sense. It is necessary that this custom be amended and the Roman customs be used. Valerius said in chapter 5 in the seventh book of his *Repulses* that the Romans whose superior government of the republic followed the order of reason had the custom that from year to year they changed nearly all the offices. And they did this so that they kept themselves from misappropriating anything without punishment, and also so that they did not become too proud. So every year they assembled the rulers of Rome, that is, those who gave out the offices, on a great square called the field of Mars,\* and there, by custom, came the powerful, the middle [class] and the humble in order to request the offices that belonged to each group. And they each had a white robe, and each put in their request for the office they asked for. So that the rulers were not deceived into giving office to those who did not deserve it, there were prudent wise men nearby to inquire into the habits and life of those requesting office and to write down how they behaved in office before.

And in this manner those who were worthy received them and those who were not were refused well and boldly. Would to God that the same was done in all countries! Everyone would give himself the trouble to be good and to acquire a good reputation. Thus, honors were distributed by the exercise of virtuous works and not by personal favoritism.

From this we have learned that in the well-governed republic certain persons should be chosen from any rank, according to their proper position, as shown before. This means that soldiers and others who belong to that group are those who are capable for military offices; and clerks and students are appropriate for the speculative sciences, philosophy, and liberal arts; likewise for other offices, as Tully said. And the good prince ought to see them as a necessity, for the honor and glory of the kingdom, the land, and the country increases most through an abundance of clerks and wise scholars, because he is well advised by them, as I said before. On which Plato said (according to the first book of the *Consolation* by Boethius\*), the republic will be very happy if the wise govern it, or else if the governors of princes study wisdom. Through this, the whole community would obey the laws and the rules of reason. And thus, as I have already often said, it would be appropriate to get rid of the presumption of many who desire honors without being worthy of them, so that the worthy are honored and receive them, and the unworthy reform themselves. And the worthy and unworthy are discerned by such practices, as is ordained by study of the sciences.

## Chapter 24 The good which comes to the prince in following the advice of the wise

Continuing this subject that the good prince ought to appreciate the wise, let us speak of the great good which comes and can come from them, such as the serious speculative philosophers, because of their sciences as well as their morals. It is written that the philosopher Archimedes,* through his good sense, maintained the peace for the city of Syracuse so that it was not captured by the Romans, and by his industry and cleverness made instruments by which the blows of military weapons were turned aside, and they could not destroy the city, yet finally it was defeated. And when the prince was inside, he asked that the philosopher not be killed. But when the soldiers went to pillage the city, a knight came to the house of Archimedes and found him writing drawings on the ground, like those of geometricians and astronomers. When he asked him what they were, he did not answer for he was most intent on what he was doing, but said only, "I beg you heartily not to disturb me in what I am doing." But he killed him. This Archimedes was a very great mathematician, so much so that some say that it was he who discovered how to square the circle. Aristotle said in his book *Predications* that it was something that while possible to understand, it could not be done in his time.

Also others said that this philosopher had foreseen his death by astrology and had announced it before the blow fell. But when someone asked him why he did not leave the place where he said he must die, he said that the movement of the heavens held him so firmly that he could not leave, from which it appears that he was of the opinion that the influence of the heavens drives one into what must become of him, which shows that he was not so great a clerk that he could not be deceived. Because this is not true with respect to the operations of the soul, which acts in freedom. It is clearly free and has liberty and power over its actions, despite whatever inclination or influence of the heavens there might be. The soul can choose which part it pleases, as Aristotle proved in his *Ethics*. And by this one can appreciate the perfect reason and knowledge of Aristotle. For on the foundation of our faith, theology has determined plainly that the will, which is free, can not be constrained by anything, otherwise sin and vice could be excused because the inclinations were constrained and dominated by force. As for the body, it is true that a human is somewhat subject by birth to the actions of the heavenly bodies, by the alternations in the courses of the heavens and also in the four primary qualities; heat, cold, dryness, and moisture. For it is not in human power that in summer one is not hot, and the other seasons are the same. But in what is subject to the soul, that is, the deliberations of the will, the influences of the heavens have no domination, despite the fact that it could be true that the action of the heavens gives many inclinations to humans, such as, for example, joviality, lechery, or other natural predispositions. But despite this, through reason, humans can put on a brake and resist following their inclinations. And it is true, said Ptolemy,* who was a great astrologer, that the wise determine the power of the stars. To prove that this saying is true, it was written about Aristotle that he was of very evil character by nature, but became temperate and well mannered through great virtue, and thus he overcame nature.

## Chapter 25 How the ancients governed themselves by philosophy

And so the good prince shall be governed by the wise, and also that he should not repudiate the science of astrology practiced by notable persons who ought to be called to privy councils, as was said before. This was proven by the philosopher Archimedes, who saved the city of Syracuse from being captured for a long time thanks to his learning, and likewise there are many other similar stories. But the good prince ought to be careful that only wise men establish his particular affairs so that he is not deceived by abusers, who by the illusion of learning simulate knowledge, but know nothing and often deceive and mislead princes and lay persons by their trickery. But when the science [of astrology] is real it can be very profitable in the maintenance and improvement of cities and kingdoms. And when there are some discreet and expert philosophers in this science, there is no doubt that they are very beneficial despite the fact that some object to this science in the council of princes. "For," as Aristotle said, "this world that is below is governed by the action of heavenly bodies," and Ptolemy said that "the images and configurations of this world below are subject to the images and configurations of the world above." And it is true that there are many descriptions of the marvels that some ancient philosophers did without error. Such people who can do so much ought to be desired in the counsels of high princes. It is not to be believed that so many of the ancient authors* would have spoken dishonestly. But nonetheless no prince should consult anyone who uses evil arts forbidden by the church, for in that lies too great a peril. Nor should he allow them nor tolerate them in his country, because too many dangers may follow. I speak only of the pure and perfect astrologers, whose science of astrology is so superior that it surpasses others in subtlety, yet it is pure, natural and without evil art or any incantations. Because of its difficulty, that is, because of its great subtlety, there are very few who are well grounded in it. And for this reason, many have blamed it because they cannot comprehend nor understand it and as is commonly said, those that are ignorant of things willingly blame them.

But to prove that the science is real and that there have been experts in it, Aristotle tells us in the first book of the *Politics* about Thales* the philosopher, whose relatives once mocked him because he did nothing but study despite being so poor that he had nothing. And when he had had enough of their arguments, he thought he would demonstrate the virtue of his knowledge and do something with his little bit of money. He knew through his knowledge of astronomy that olives would be plentiful that year and that the next year there would be very few. So he bought a very large quantity which he sold the next year at a very high price, and thus he made a great profit. Thus, Aristotle said, he showed his relations that it was an easy thing for a philosopher to become rich. But philosophers desire another kind of happiness, that is, of understanding, which others value little. On this subject, an astrologer called Spiromia foresaw the death of Julius Caesar* at Rome, through his science. When the time was near, Julius Caesar said to Spiromia, "Do you not know that the Ides of March have nearly passed?" (That was the time he had foreseen.) The other answered, "Don't you know they have not passed yet!" And so on the last of those thirty days, Julius Caesar was killed at the Capitol by the faction of Brutus and Cassius and many other senators, who gave him more than twenty-two stab wounds, as Orosius testifies in his fifth book of the *History*. And so the amazing and pitiful death of this high prince took place.

## Chapter 26 How it is suitable for a prince to be prudent and wise in eloquence

As we have said, it is necessary for the good prince to be a good judge, and also good that he love and attract sages and philosophers to him. Certainly it is expedient that he be wise himself and know something of the sciences, about which the aforementioned Valerius said that the science of astrology was very profitable to the republic, and especially in battles.

Supplicius Gallus' serious study of all kinds of liberal arts saved his people from sudden fear by his knowledge. He led a very large quantity of soldiers against the king of Persia, when during a calm night, the moon disappeared suddenly, that is, lost its light because of an eclipse. His army was astonished and lost all hope of victory in battle. But Supplicius very wisely showed them the cause of the eclipse in the movement of the heavens and reassured them, showing them that it was a natural event.

Similarly, it is written in the *History of Alexander* that because of just such a thing, his army was astonished and mutinous against him, because they thought it was a punishment for the wrongs he had done. But Aristanus, a wise knight who knew astrology, put their minds at peace.

For this reason it can well be said that the wise king of France, Charles V, who governed himself always through great learning, particularly loved philosophers of the science of astrology. Out of love of it, he studied astrology himself till he understood the science sufficiently. That it is appropriate for the prince to be wise is supported by the saying of Plato, which Valerius repeats. Even though brief, nonetheless it is very great and excellent saying: "the world will be happy when the wise begin to rule, or kings begin to be wise." Since every branch of learning is a part of science, it is most suitable in a prince to learn to speak well and wisely and to give his reasons in an logical fashion. Because there is no doubt that wise and well-ordered speech out of the mouth of the prince is more weighty and willingly heard than when it comes from another. And also it can be to his benefit, in various cases, for there is hardly any bold spirit that is not softened by fair words.

It is written of Philocrates that he was so eloquent a man that despite the ancients being governed by wise philosophers and having the custom of living in liberty without a ruler, so great was his wise and gentle eloquence that he was made prince and ruler of Athens, despite the opposition of the wise Solon who supported liberty. There are other examples to show how often beautiful eloquence is of great help.

But to eloquence, which is called rhetoric, Valerius also joined the kind of bodily movement in speaking. When eloquence is combined with gentle movement of the body, it affects the listeners in three ways: it affects the spirit of some and the ears of others, and it seduces and sweetens the eyes of others. Gestures affect the spirit, he said, when by suitable motion of the body, the speaker represents things and brings them to memory, like dangers, fortune and misfortune, virtues, vices, examples of the great, and the effects of counsels, by which things, spirits are involved and give their consent to the speaker. Secondly, by suitable and well-moderated pronunciation, the ears of the auditors are invaded and conquered by great pleasure and delight. Thirdly, the eyes of those that see it are conquered in that they see and consider the handsome and honest countenance of the persuader or speaker, and thus his eloquence is enriched by these things. And by its opposite, he says, the speaker is displeasing and of little virtue, and thus has less effect. For example, said Valerius, Quintus Ortensius worked so hard to study beautiful movement of the body, more or as much as beautiful speech, that one never knew whether people came to hear him or see him speak, and thus, said Valerius, sight serves the words of the orator or the speaker, and words serves the sight of the listeners.

46

## Chapter 27 How it is a suitable thing for a prince to have good bearing

With fair words and frank movement of the body, fair eloquence and honorable bearing also suit princes. And the thing which is most pleasant is to see a fair and superior presence in the prince, not arrogance but wisdom, and it will be of great benefit to him who naturally has it or acquires it by knowing how to temper his manners. As it is said of Pericles the Wise, of whom I have spoken, that he was of such noble eloquence and bearing that through his wise speech, he made the Athenians (even if it was hard for them to follow his orders) do everything he desired. And then on the subject of fair eloquence in the prince and handsome carriage and bearing, we have examples from ancient foreigners of pleasant and ornate speech. But it is not right, it seems to me, to forget our French princes, especially those that we have seen and see daily with our own eyes; they are very special and excellent in the adornment of fair eloquence, as was the very illustrious, knowledgeable, wise, and prudent King Charles V, who was spoken of before, who was without fault, and with great wisdom. It was a great pleasure to see his fair and lordly bearing, and hear his eloquent language. And whether in council or elsewhere, he would explain his reasons so well that he never failed to put his premises in good order and to deduce to the conclusion by varied points, and then concluded in his intention very nobly. He demonstrated this in front of his uncle the emperor, the time that he was at Paris. He described before the council, at length, one after the other, the wrongs that were done by the king of England, and that he wanted to recommence the war (as I have described in the third part of the book of his deeds and good manners, near the end of the book).

And this very noble quality of speech, without doubt descended to his very excellent son Louis, duke of Orleans. As everyone knows, it is a marvelous thing to hear him speak in council or with other groups in such a beautiful and polished fashion that even the famous clerks of the University of Paris – perfect rhetoricians – when they happened to hear him, were amazed by his speech.

For if he proposes first to bring up the question or the fact on which he wants to speak, there is no point he fails to make, and all his points are appropriate. And if he answers another, no matter how strange and varied the subject before him, he does not fail to give all the principle points and aspects of the subject and answers each point so carefully that those who hear cross themselves because they marvel at his great memory, beautiful rhetoric, and his eloquence and bodily movements which correspond to the noble language used, so that he can well be compared to the ancients mentioned above.

Also the very excellent duke of Burgundy, Philip, brother of the before mentioned King Charles, and uncle of Louis, had, with the great knowledge for which he was known, the most beautiful speech and very gracious eloquence. So I conclude, in my opinion, that such eloquence and richness of language, though it comes to some by nature more than others by learning, is a sign of good understanding, steadfast thought, and constant courage which are most useful in a high prince and a worthy man.

## Chapter 28 How the good prince ought to be diligent and occupy himself with the needs of his country

Returning to the subject of the third point mentioned before that the good prince maintains justice and grounds himself in following it, let us to look at what things are proper to him for good living. But seeing the quantity of virtues which remain to speak of, all of which he ought to have, it would be too long to describe each separately. Let us say more generally how the good prince ought always to be busy with virtuous works, despite the fact that it seems to ignorant folks that his majesty the prince has nothing to do except live at rest and at ease, in luxury and honors, because he has enough ministers to do everything! But without doubt, this is not true, because there is no other man who has such hard work to do if he wants to live justly as a prince should. If he is wise, the office of rule where God has established him is burden-some. He has to know the deeds of his ministers, for if they do wrong the punishment and the blame come to the prince for his negligence, to the soul as well as his body. Thus, since varied affairs of the kingdom and the country are numerous, there will be no leisure for him if he wants to do his work properly. Ah, how noble a thing it is in a prince to have a just occupation and to flee lazy negligence, exactly as for the rest of the people! As a valiant Roman said, it was of more benefit to Rome when they were busy, even in warfare, than in idleness. For very powerful kingdoms were brought to virtue by exertion, and too great rest leads to the vices of leisure. And on the subject (that the business and care caused by war is in sometimes profitable to the morals of the young) Valerius has these words: "Truly, being burdened by war, which is a terrible word, has maintained and sustained the high morals of our city, Rome, and rest, which is a sweet and soft word, has filled Rome with many vices."

On this subject, Justin* said in his first book, that when Cyrus,* the king of Persia had finally conquered the people of the kingdom of Lydia, who were always rebelling, he believed that he had no better method of keeping them subjugated than by introducing pleasures. He wanted to give them leisure and to keep them at bodily ease, and so he forbade them to use weapons and commanded that they play and amuse themselves with all kinds of gambling, and accustom themselves to merchandise, and all such things, and that they have all kinds of leisure. And so these people, who had been so powerful and brave in arms, became as soft and dainty as women. So they were conquered by pleasures when they could not be by arms. On this subject, Valerius tells us that the city in Africa called Carthage was so chivalrous and noble that it troubled Romans in war for a long time before it was finally destroyed. Quintus Metellus, a most worthy Roman knight said before the Senate that he did not know whether the victory over Carthage was more profitable or detrimental for Rome, for they would lose the noble knight Hannibal, whose coming to Italy forced the Romans – who had been asleep before – to exercise in arms. So now, he was fearful that having been relieved of so strong and eager an enemy they would go back to sleep and lose their virtue. Vegetius* said in the third book, that the good duke, that is, the good captain, ought to desire wartime more than peacetime. For rest makes knights and soldiers weak and slothful and yet the exercise and work of arms makes them tough and able.

## Chapter 29 How the good prince ought to love and honor his gentlemen and his knights

Because everything cannot be said at once, it is suitable to delay some subjects, and talk about them one after the other. So that the nobles and knights may marvel, who up to this point have seen and read the present writing on the government of the good prince, I have divided this book into three parts, as said before, in which I say how to govern and rule. I have not yet discussed their estate, not because I was ignorant of it or forgot the good, honor and great love that the good prince ought to have particularly for them. But in excusing myself in this, saving their reverence, I say truly that it is not by forgetting, or ignorance or not knowing their dignity and reputation, but to keep place and time in my volume to speak more worthily of their authority. Because my purpose brings us to the subject of battle, let us say how the good prince who desires to exercise the right of justice (that is render to each in his power that which is his due); it is a worthy obligation to the rank of knighthood – that is, the worthy nobles who carry arms – love, honor, and very great reward. Oh what a noble, honorable and profitable thing it is in the kingdom, empire, or country to have brave knights, that is, good soldiers!

Are they not the guardians of the prince and the people of the country, and the champions that shed their blood and life for the honor of the prince and the public good? Who could reward them enough expensive provisions, sufficient praise, or render the grace and merit which is fitting a worthy man of integrity, experienced in arms, noble in manners and condition, loyal in deed and in courage, wise in government and diligent in chivalrous pursuits?! Alas, such people are scarcely rewarded according to their merits in France. For if they were honored as they were due, 100 more would follow in their steps. The valiant Romans did, for without doubt, of all the good and wise customs that have been established, those of Rome caused them to become conquerors of the whole world. There is no doubt that with the exercise of arms their wisdom was a great help to them. Therefore one could think that the Romans were better and more worthy than other people. But without doubt, it was because that they knew better than any other how to recognize the good and highly reward their deeds. They studied ways to give a reason to do well in this. And so, on their manner of honoring these worthy knights, I will begin with what Valerius says, first on their princes and sovereigns, then, I will talk about other knights.

At the time of the glory of Romans, they had a custom at Rome that when the princes (that is the highest captains and leaders of their great army), were victorious in the conquest of a kingdom that was well managed and difficult to conquer (as was Scipio Africanus, who subjugated Africa and the noble city of Carthage or Pompey the Great who conquered many kingdoms, or Julius Caesar, or many other conquerors), when they returned to Rome after these noble victories, the Romans had established a certain honor, called a "triumph" which gave them honor when these princes entered the city. Isidore* said that this was due for complete victory. And it was called a triumph, said Valerius, first because "try" means three and "umph" means "his power"; because to have a triumph was given only after three votes, that is, three different judgments. The first judgment came from soldiers who had experienced both the ordeal and the victory, because they knew the deed and so they could judge it. Secondly, there was a written report to the Senate (that is, the princes of Rome who sat on the council) and according to the facts, they judged if the person had deserved a triumph. The third was the consent of the common voice of the people.

Following the judgment they took a richly adorned chariot and everyone went out of the city to meet him, dressed in rich robes, according to their rank. He who was being given the triumph was seated on the elaborately adorned chariot, which signified glory and honor. Then he was most reverently greeted by the other princes and everyone generally did him reverence. Then if he had fought and won in combat the princes crowned him with palm for the palm has thorns. If he had won by strategy and by strength without great losses of his own, he was crowned with laurel which smells sweet and is always in virtue. And this was the most proper triumph and joyous victory, for according to Isidore, victory is not joyous when accompanied by great losses. This is why Sallust* praises princes who have victory without the slaughter of their people and their own flesh.

In front of this triumphal chariot, the prisoners were brought, who were often very famous kings and great princes, as well as the pack animals which carried the treasure into Rome. Nearest the chariot went those who had fought the best and who carried the most tokens of victory and great deeds. The tokens of victory were jewels of various kinds that were given them according to their deeds, and which they had to wear if they had fought and were victorious. They were given their own jewel accordingly, if, for example in the assault on a castle, he conducted himself so valiantly that the castle was taken, he was given one kind of jewel, and another if, for example, he was engaged in hand-to-hand combat, or another feat of arms. Jewels were established for all kinds of deeds. Thus, those who took a city were given a crown of gold. Other deeds meant collars, helmets, belts, garters, or bracelets of gold. Jewels were established for all manner of feats, and these jewels had to be worn openly or otherwise they were taken back. This was because the Romans wanted them seen as an example, so that they could not be reproached for wearing it by ambition or arrogance, because they just followed their orders, and to wear these things was a great honor, for each could see the merit of the other, and the more good they had done the more they were honored by all who came, and no one could wear them unless they won them by arms. Would to God that France, which is the most noble land in the world, had such a custom! I believe that there would be some who were less handsome and some who would be more handsome than there are now! Thus, the most valiant went nearest the chariot with the princes of Rome by its side. The people went in front and the officers came after according to their rank. After the chariot came the soldiers who had been at the victory, who were honored and feasted most grandly by the Romans, and in this manner they entered the city of Rome.

## Chapter 30 How the good prince ought to avoid lechery

As was said before, the good prince and honest judge ought not be idle nor occupy himself with too many pleasures, consequently he should avoid lechery. For as the authors all tell us, idleness is the food of carnal lusts. This vice of lechery is despicable in the prince, and can be the cause of decline in his prosperity, may shame him, and cause other inconveniences. In this we have the example of Sardanapolon, king of the Assyrians, who lost his kingdom shamefully. Also a king of France was dethroned for the same reason, and the same can be said of many others. Valerius says that there was a city in Campania called Capua that was so given to pleasures and lechery that it corrupted and poisoned Hannibal and all his army. Titus Livius* says in the third book of the third decade,* that after Hannibal had won a variety of great battles in Italy, he went to Capua and was absorbed and involved in frequenting women, and the ease and pleasures of the body, with wines and fine foods, and entertainment to which he was not accustomed to indulge in excessively. Afterwards, neither he nor his army was eager to endure the great labor to which they had been accustomed. This mistake took all the strength of his knights away and they forgot their old discipline. Thus, he said, he came out of Capua a different man from when he entered it. And so, said Valerius, the pride and the cruelty of Africa and of Carthage, which could not be defeated by arms, was broken, brought down by pleasures, by which the victorious Hannibal and his army were defeated and corrupted. Valerius said "Oh what thing is more damaging than voluptuousness and pleasures by which virtue is extinguished and victory annihilated!" On the corruption of Hannibal, Seneca writes in a letter which he sent to his disciple Lucillus saying that the nourishment of Campania made Hannibal soft. He conquered them by arms, but he was conquered by luxury.

Valerius also says that the death of the worthy prince Epaminondas was the beginning of deterioration of the Athenians' virtue and strength. For when they had lost the person who had often forced them into great battles, and who often defeated them, and whom they envied because his bravery; they became lazy, and they no longer supported their soldiers, either on sea or on land, but spent their funds on feasts and games, and turned the deeds of their predecessors into songs. And it sufficed them to write histories about the wars but do nothing, and so the high reputation of Greece fell until the time of Philip, father of Alexander, who brought it up again.

# Chapter 31 How the good prince should govern himself

Because anger is a very natural vice, and attracts hatred, and sometimes causes powerful men to be cruel, it pleases me to give an example to show that a good prince ought to control himself from something so repugnant and degrading. Valerius describes this as a vice, and even spoke to princes thus: "Often persons, especially when they are high and powerful, commit great cruelties through impetuous hatred." And in order to help better understand the qualities of these two passions, he distinguishes them, saying that wrath and hatred resemble each other in that both are violent and trouble the spirit of one who is angry and hateful, and make him desire vengeance. But there are many differences between the two, as Aristotle says in the second book of *Rhetoric*. It suffices to speak of two at present: The first is that where anger is avenged, it is sufficient, and the person is appeased. But hatred desires the destruction and extermination of all that is hated, it can not be satisfied, but rather hatred grows.

Secondly, the wrathful person desires to appear angry with him on whom he desires revenge, and wants no harm to come to him without his knowing the source. And because of this the wrathful person does harm publicly, and not in secret. But the hateful person prefers to harm secretly rather than publicly, and because of this, hatred is worse than simple wrath. It seems to me that anger can exist without hatred but hatred cannot exist without anger. These two kinds of misbehavior conduct one to cruelty, and nothing is more reprehensible in a prince than to be cruel.

To increase the lessons that the prince ought to learn from this, it pleases me to quote from Valerius on the deformities that result (thanks to God in his mercy and to Him is the glory, our princes of France and of the noble royal blood are all born with a good nature, and it seems to me, are better behaved than lesser persons in the kingdom, or any prince of any other nation in the world, which is a praiseworthy thing in such noble blood).

Certainly, Valerius said that the habit of cruelty is horrible: one's appearance is cruel, one's spirit is violent, one's voice is terrible. Everything about it is full of menace and cruel commands. And if one asks a cruel person to cease or to hold his tongue, that enflames his cruelty even more. Cruelty hesitates at no pain, and will not be restrained, and others naturally hate it, for cruelty, he says, is a disposition repugnant to civil conversation, to which civility we are naturally inclined, as Aristotle said in the first book of the *Politics*. And everything which is against nature, by nature it is our inclination to hate.

Let these things be a mirror for the prince, in which to look at himself, and all others should do so as well. For let us suppose that there was one of these vices to which one were naturally inclined. If the person does not learn how to master himself, and conquer it, it is a sign that he is not virtuous, and a person without virtue is not worthy of honor.

## Chapter 32 How it is proper for the good prince to take his recreation in any honest diversion after his great labor

So that my intention be clearly understood, and so that I not be proved to be mistaken in my present work, when I said that the prince ought to be busy all the time; these words should not be taken absolutely, because one would not want the prince to be extremely over burdened. This is not my intent and so I say that the prince and likewise all who are burdened with high and important occupations must sometimes cease work and rest in leisure. And on this Valerius, whose words are more authoritative than mine, said on this subject: there are two kinds of idleness of which one ought to be avoided. This one causes virtue to disappear and makes life foolish and impotent in all good works, and renders one inclined to lust and accompanies the inclination to sensuality. Ovid* spoke of this kind of idleness in his book the *Remedy of Love*: "If you put aside your idleness, the arts of the God of love are lost."

The other idleness I understand to be without vice. It is virtuous, and sometimes through it virtue may be acquired. It is sometimes appropriate for nobles and excellent men for the restoration of their natural vigor, so that the moderate cessation of labor, makes them more lively for work. For this moderate idleness recreates the natural virtues and strengthens them for better work. And so Ovid said, "he who has no rest cannot endure long by nature."

Valerius gives the example of Scipio and Lelius who were hard-working and worthy knights, who were such good companions and friends, that just as they were companions in the hardest labor, so they were in rest, in idleness, and in recreation, amusing themselves in honest sports, when it was time for them to play.

## Chapter 33 How the good prince who knows that he does his duty in all virtue ought reasonably to desire praise and glory

Now it is time to bring to an end the first part of my book, on the introduction of princes to a virtuous life. For an abyss could be filled with all the sayings and stories of good habits which a prince should cultivate. But it seems to me better to exclude length by speaking generally of all the virtues. If he followed those discussed here, then

55

there would be songs of glory and praise about him like once greeted the great and worthy prince of Athens Themistocles*! Once it happened that singers of songs and ancient epics came before him. One of the knights asked him in jest what song would be most pleasing to hear. He answered "The one that says truly that I am virtuous and that I have done good and noteworthy deeds." Thus a well-conducted prince is worthy of praise, but the one who does not act virtuously does not have willing praise from the common estimation, but only in what he merits. It should not surprise us if the one who is worthy, virtuous and who does good deeds is praised for them! For it is known, according to the ancients, that high princes and noblemen of times past were greedy for glory and that they had the desire to acquire such glory by virtue, as one can see by their worthy deeds. It appears quite natural that everyone desires his own perfection, and so the person who is sovereign over all worldly creatures desires the testimony and proof of his perfection. And as the Philosopher says, glory and honor bring reverence, which shows that one has in him the dignity that is shown, and the desire to be honored is rooted and joined to human nature. But not everyone desires the pain of acquiring it. And the means by which honor and praise should be acquired is virtuous works, says the Philosopher. No other means is worthy of glory, as Tully says in the first book of *On Duties*. Despite what anyone says, everyone ought to be honored because of virtue and living well. No honor, praise or worldly glory is sufficient reward for virtuous deeds and excellence. According to Aristotle, one can lawfully desire a reward for good deeds to attract others to similar virtues. And Tully says that one scarcely finds anyone who after great and virtuous labors does not desire glory and honor as part of his reward. And because of such honor and glory, Aristotle says (in the third book of *Ethics*) the strength and great courage of virtuous men is identified and proven, who by their deeds have been honored. The unworthy and vicious ones are despised and blamed. But Socrates said that those who chose the way of glory just had to show by their deeds that they were as everyone would be believed, which means good. Socrates warns of those who have the appearance of right and virtue without the deeds, as hypocrites do. So the good prince who desires to reach paradise, as well as glory and praise in the world from all people, will love God and fear God above everything. And he will love the public good of his kingdom or country more than his own as well. He ought to do justice without hindrance and to justly render to each his own according to the power which is his. As justice commands he will be humane, generous, and merciful to his dependents as was described before. And in doing so, he will acquire praise through his good merits, not only during his life, but eternally, as Valerius said about the excellent prince Julius Caesar, who by his merits and good deeds after his death was reputed to be a god. For the ancients of old, who did not yet have the faith, when they saw a person, a man or woman who surpassed others in any superiority of grace, believed that such virtue could not be without divine virtue. And Julius Caesar had many great virtues. Above all others, he was just and merciful. They said that such virtue in a man could not perish in leaving life, and his soul ascended to heaven, deified.

Here ends the first part of this book.

# PART TWO

# On Knights and Nobles

Here begins the second part of this book, which addresses chivalrous nobles

## Chapter 1 The first chapter describes how these nobles are the arms and hands of the body politic

Having concluded speaking to princes whom we described according to Plutarch as the head of the living image of the body politic and exhorting them to a virtuous life, it is appropriate in this second part of the present book to keep our promise and speak of the arms and hands of this image which, according to Plutarch, are the nobles, knights, and all those of their estate. In order to follow the style already begun, we ought to discuss their introduction to virtue and good manners, and particularly to deeds of chivalry, for they are responsible for guarding the public, according to the writings of the authors.* While the same virtue is just as appropriate and necessary for the ordinary person, the simple knight, or the noble, as for princes, nevertheless, the estates differ in their way of life, in their conversation, and kinds of activity; thus it is suitable for my treatment of the subject to differ as well. The thing that is appropriate for the prince to do is not appropriate for the simple knight or the noble, and likewise the opposite. But there is no doubt that one can speak the same to nobles as to princes when it concerns the aforementioned virtues. This means that it is also their part to love God and fear Him above all else, to care for the public good for which they were

established, to preserve and love justice according to their compet-
ences; just as it is for princes and other human beings. To be
humane, liberal, and merciful, to love the wise and good and to
govern by their advice, and likewise they should have all the other
virtues, which I do not think I will describe for them, as it suffices
to have described them once. What I have said before concerning
the virtues serves each estate in the polity, and each individual person,
therefore I will not proceed much longer in this form. For it is sufficient to speak of the manner in which everyone ought to do his own
part in the order that God has established, that is, nobles do as nobles
should, the populace does as it is appropriate for them, and everyone
should come together as one body of the same polity, to live justly
and in peace as they ought. That is what I had in mind when I was
speaking of teaching them good morals. So I will begin my subject,
as I did in the beginning of the first part where I spoke of the way
to educate the children of princes. Now I will begin by speaking on
how the ancient nobles educated their children, as it is written in
their histories.

## Chapter 2 How the ancient nobles educated their children

In the chapter on the customs in which the ancient nobles educated
their sons, Valerius said that as soon as they were grown enough that
they could endure hardship, they were taken from their mother's
entourage and made to exercise according to their abilities and physical development, and very quickly at this age they accustomed them
to bear armor according to their strength, and to wear armor in some
exercises that were not too hard and difficult. They were not fed with
dainty foods nor fancy clothing as many are today, but given plain
food. As to their dress, there was a proper sort of clothing that nobles
wore but no one else, but I do not believe that this was trimmed in
martin fur nor embroidered. Also they accustomed them to sleep on
hard beds, to go to bed late and to get up early, and to other bearable
discomforts that were appropriate to life in arms. And in this manner,
the ancients brought up their children to become very admirable
men, as is revealed by their deeds. It does justify and confirm some
gentle folk in Germany and elsewhere who allow little arrogance in
their children, but make them serve other gentle folk and be their

pages, travelling with them and enduring many hardships. I believe that when they are grown they are never the worse for it, and that gentlemen thus brought up are wise, able in military deeds, and more capable than those brought up to be elegant and delicate. Vegetius in *On Chivalry*, said that those who are accustomed to work do well at arms.

And as for feeding them, some say that the child nourished on fine wines and foods will have better blood, and as a consequence will be stronger. That opinion is false, because dainty foods are earlier corrupted than others, according to Aristotle, nor do they strengthen a person's body as well as plain foods do. And we see this in our own experience, for the Bretons* and the Normans* are commonly fed plain food and they are not refined in their food and drink, but they are commonly stronger and tougher than other people. Because of this they are willingly hired as mercenaries as are the Burgundians,* and also other nations which are not accustomed to dainties. And the ancients, especially the Romans, brought up their children, as Valerius says, in good manners and kept them in fear and under obedience, which is very wise. According to what is written in the *Book of Twelve Errors*, the third level of error is that of the disobedient young man who ought to be helpful, submissive, and humble. For just as one never finds fruit on trees where there were never any blossoms, so a person will never acquire honor who has not labored in his youth in obedience and discipline. And about this humility of the children of nobles, Valerius says, youths used to render honor to the elderly as if they were their parents. When elderly nobles went to the councils and the courts of princes, the young accompanied them, waited on them, standing most humbly until they returned, and thus they were toughened to endure hardship. The elderly went to great trouble to teach them good manners and to give them a good example, through which good advice and habits, they became noble, virtuous, and well mannered. And afterwards, following their custom, they were named to the offices of the nobility by their elders who knew them well. And these were the customs of the nobles with their children: and they had the highest reputation for their patience, virtue, and endurance. Valerius said that when they had any festivals and the young happened to be there, when they came to sit at the tables, they asked carefully who was coming, so that they were ready to serve any old person who came. They did not seat themselves first,

and their tables* were taken up first, and they had to present themselves to the old, which means, says Valerius, that they got used to
speaking little, which is a very good habit in young people. According
to Anselm,* in the book *On Similitudes*, a young man has three things
which ought to be recommended in him; modesty of the heart, abstin-
ence of the body, and silence of the mouth (which means to speak
little), because according to the sage, if the fool holds his tongue he
may be taken for wise!

## Chapter 3 Examples of the learning that the ancients gave their children

Now we have said how the Romans of old taught their children in
youth, so it is suitable to tell what followed this teaching, that is, the
effects on their worth when they came of age, as example of virtue
in children. Valerius tells us that often in the childhood of a person,
one perceives his disposition and good manners. So he tells of a
noble Roman child named Emilius Lepidus* who learned instruction
in arms so well, and delighted in it so much that he wanted to be
armed in a battle. Despite the nature of children, which is fearful of
seeing the horrors of war, Valerius says that he fought so well that
the princes of the council of Rome listed him in the register of their
noble deeds, as a great marvel. Also, because of the encouragement
to virtue given by the noble to the children, their dispositions were
inclined to compassion, good nature, and firm courage. Valerius tells
of another noble child whose tutor took him to school. When he saw
the cruelest of the princes of Rome, named Sulla, who in his cruelty
had cut off the heads of many Romans, the child asked his master
how such a tyrant could exist without someone murdering him. The
master answered that there were plenty of those who wanted to, but
he had too many guards. Then, said the child, if someone would give
him a knife, it would be done because he saw him every day, and he
would not fail to kill him. With that, the master no longer allowed
him to see him (considering the great courage of the child) without
searching him for a knife.

Also, on the subject of the great courage of the well brought up
child, Valerius tells of a most noble man of Rome, who brought up
a son with such great rigor that he drove him away from himself.
Although everything ought to be moderate, he showed him such great

rudeness, that the child did not dare go into his presence. There was another powerful man in Rome who hated the child's father (I do not know why) so he plotted to injure him financially, so that the other would begin to overspend his means. The good child, his son, paid no attention to the rudeness and hurt he had received from his father, because the natural love which he had would not allow him to tolerate the torment of his father. So he took a knife in secret, and went to his father's enemy and told him that he wanted to speak to him privately. The other, who was a man of the council, what we would call an advocate,* assumed that the child wanted his advice in some undertaking against his father, and was happy. So he brought him into his office secretly. When the child saw that they were alone, he closed the door, seized the old man by the throat, threw him on the floor under him, and said he would kill him immediately if he did not promise to leave his father in peace and make amends for the burdens that he had placed on him. And he was so terrified by these few words that he not only promised, but also kept his promise.

## Chapter 4 How the noble knights of old promoted the youths that they had taught

As you have heard, the children of Rome profited from the good examples and teaching given them by the elders. And the older men who are bad examples to the young must be reprimanded. Some old fools are hardened in their bad habits and filthy customs, and do not restrain themselves at all in front of the young, but make them their messengers to bring them their foolish news. It certainly is a great abuse when those who ought to be teachers of good doctrine are examples of villainy. And there is nothing in the world as unseemly to see as an old man without virtue or sense. And as is said about the noble Romans of old who governed themselves so wisely in everything: they had so much delight in the good deeds of the young that when they saw their virtues, they did not deter them from holding high dignities or offices. Even though they were young in age, they considered their virtue and sense. As we saw, wise Scipio Africanus was only twenty-four when he was made head of a large army, which was not customarily given before the age of thirty. But they did not find themselves disappointed for he behaved with greatness and the

Romans benefited by acquiring all of Africa, Carthage and the major part of Spain, where he did marvelous deeds.

Similarly Pompey the Great as a young child demonstrated so much virtue and nobility that at the age of twenty-two, the Romans made him consul, that is [leader] of a great army. He displayed himself so well in the office and dignity, that he earned many triumphs in his time, which was the highest honor he could have as was described in the first part of this book. He was awarded the triumph for defeating Mithridates,* the king of Pontus who had been so powerful that he defeated twenty-two countries of [different] languages that had afflicted the Romans in battle over forty years. He also had the triumph over King Tigranes of Armenia, mentioned before, and many other kings, cities and countries, which he brought under obedience to Rome (as many as twenty-two kingdoms), and for brief time, all the regions which are between the Caucasus mountains and the Red Sea. He also purged the sea of a great multitude of pirates who occupied the parts of the seacoast of Europe and Asia. And so the schools described above produced students such as this. And for examples I will tell you more particularly of the chivalrous deeds of these good pupils and disciples.

## Chapter 5 How there are six good conditions that are necessary for nobles and knights, and the first of the six

It seems to me that according to the writings of the authors on the manners* of noblemen, six conditions are especially necessary if they desire honor due for their merits. Otherwise their nobility is nothing but a mockery. The first is that they ought to love arms and the art of them perfectly, and they ought to practice that work. The second condition is that they ought to be very bold, and have such firmness and constancy in their courage that they never flee nor run from battles out of fear of death, nor spare their blood nor life, for the good of their prince and the safe keeping of their country and the republic. Otherwise they will endure capital punishment through sentence of the law, and be dishonored forever.

Thirdly, they ought to give heart and steadiness to each other, counselling their companions to do well, and to be firm and steadfast.

The fourth is to be truthful and to uphold their fealty and oath. Fifthly, they ought to love and desire honor above all worldly things. Sixthly, they ought to be wise and crafty against their enemies and in all deeds of arms. To those who observe them and keep these conditions well there will be honor. But it is no doubt more difficult to do these things than it is to speak of them! Therefore, Aristotle said that the greatest honor is found where the greatest difficulty is.

On the first condition that the noble ought to have, which is to love and practice arms, and keep them right, we can give the examples of many noble knights. But since we have begun with the history of the Romans, let us continue with them, for it seems to me that they particularly loved warfare, and as a consequence were very noble (that is, the good ones who are mentioned in the writings of the ancient authors where their deeds are told). And although they loved arms well, they also observed knightly discipline, that is they kept right in suitable things by rules, so that they failed in nothing. Those who broke the established rules were punished. Valerius said that the discipline of chivalry, that is, keeping the rules and order appropriate to it, was the highest honor and firm foundation of the empire of Rome. Moreover, he said that they won their great victories, they secured the state, and the certain position of happy peace and tranquility because they kept this discipline well. Valerius gives us many examples of how they kept their discipline. Among others, he tells of a great rebellion in Sicily against the Romans. A consul, that is, one of their princes or high captains, was sent before a great army. He was called Calpurnius Piso. He sent one of his captains to lead a company of soldiers to guard a port against his enemies. But he was surprised by a great multitude of these people so that he and his army were forced to give up their arms. When Calpurnius the consul heard of this it seemed to him that they had not had sufficient watch guards, so when he [the captain] returned he shamed him publicly: he had him dressed in the clothing that the nobles wore, which was called a "toga," and as a sign that he had dishonored his nobility by giving himself up so easily, he had the fringe taken off, and forbade him to ride as long as the army did. And he was not allowed to stay with the other knights, that is, soldiers mounted on horseback, of whom he was captain. And he and his men were placed among the slingers, who were mere boys and foot soldiers, of no price,* who used slings.

## Chapter 6 More on the first good condition

Valerius describes how the Romans spared no one who did wrong no matter how good or notable in order to keep this discipline. He tells of a knight named Fabius Rustilanus who was master and captain of a great army of Romans. He was victor over a great army of the enemy, but won without having permission of the dictator or the consul who was his ruler. He was beaten with rods and stripped naked. And yet it was great grace that they did not do worse to him, but because he was a brave knight they did not. Valerius said these piteous words about him: "Fabius Rustilanus gave his powerful and victorious flesh and blood to be torn by the executioner's rods, shedding the blood and opening the wounds that he had suffered in his glorious victories."

In this fashion, the Romans kept their discipline so that they were feared. On this subject, Valerius tells of a noble consul who was slain in battle, despite the fact that his side won the war and gained the victory. The Romans were informed that the solders had failed to save him, and had let their leader be killed, because they had not been sufficiently far forward of the arrows and lances of their enemies to save their prince. The senators of Rome, Valerius said, ordered that these men not be paid either in wages or in kind for the year.

Likewise, the Carthaginians who were such noble soldiers put their captains to dolorous death when they gave bad orders in their wars and battles. Even if the venture went well, they said that no one deserves glory or praise for anything he has done but that one should be punished if one did something without reason. When Valerius had finished speaking of the discipline of knighthood, he concluded that the Romans conquered the most exalted of kings, mastered the high Alps, and achieved marvelous adventures, because they kept their discipline nor could they have accomplished all this without discipline.

## Chapter 7 On the second condition

When speaking of the boldness which is the second good condition that is necessary in a good soldier, the authors say that it is a virtue that comes from the great soul [magna anima] that the clerics call "magnanimity" without which no human strength accomplishes great deeds. Boldness often achieves more than great physical strength does. Often times one sees a small man, weak and thin of body, who is of such strong courage and so bold that he will dare to take arms against a very strong and big man, and sometimes vanquishes him. The Emperor Alexander was one of the smallest men known, yet he once beat King Porus of India in hand-to-hand combat, although he was a bigger and stronger man than most others. In his great boldness, Alexander dared to undertake world conquest, and achieved it, which is a marvelous thing. And others have achieved by their boldness such marvels that they seemed impossible to do, for Ovid said, "the gods help the bold" and writes in his poem about the god, Mars,* who helped a young knight because of his boldness. When he fought another who was much stronger than he, Mars launched a stone against the stronger one, and hit him in the face, which knocked him down, so that the weak conquered the strong. (It might have been true that someone threw a stone which killed this person by chance, and the foolish people of this time did not know where it came from, and so they thought it was thrown by the god Mars to aid the other. I do not know.)

Also Valerius said that the god Mars similarly helped a Roman knight who fought against another, by sending a crow to help him, who scratched the face of his adversary with his beak and talons. These stories are told because often Fortune is good to the bold, sending them lucky events that seem to come like miracles in many cases. But nevertheless, to speak properly, boldness – the pure and proper honorable boldness which should be praised – is that which is based on reason, and on things that are possible and reasonable to do, not undertaking something that is very likely to be wrong out of presumption and foolhardiness. This cannot have a good result, for example, such as one man against many, or when a few people attack a great force of the enemy, or when one person does many outrageous things and believes no one will dare avenge them. Such boldness will not last long. When sometimes by chance it seems that the enterprise is good, the next day it will destroy its master and those who believe him, and there will be no honor, because it is considered folly and presumption. For as was said before, the discipline of knighthood is not found everywhere. When there is neither temperance nor moderation an act is not praiseworthy. Sometimes by chance something good seems to come of it, but nevertheless it will bring evil in the end.

## Chapter 8 More on the same subject and Roman examples

It is true that boldness comes from great courage, and therefore we ought to continue to give examples of our subject. The very excellent and noble conqueror, Julius Caesar had by his knightly discipline instructed his knights and soldiers in the boldness and great courage which good soldiers ought to have, so as not to flee the battle from fear of death nor be found cowards. Valerius describes a noble knight of Julius Caesar who was named Marcus Cesius, whose feats of arms in battle were so marvelous that a great number of people were sent to overpower him. But he killed anyone who approached him. He showed his strength and the boldness of his great courage even more, suffering such a blow in the eye that it was knocked out of his head. But despite that, he seemed not to have any pain, nor did he leave the battle, either for that wound or any other. He never stopped fighting until he fell dead on the mound of men he had killed. His shield was found pierced in 120 places. In praise of him, Valerius says, Julius Caesar nourished and brought up his knights on his discipline, that is, on the exhortations, examples, and practice which he showed them.

Valerius tells of another of Julius Caesar's knights called Altilius who once was in a great sea battle against Marseilles, in which his right hand was cut off. But he never backed off nor left the battle because of the pain but took his sword in his left hand and fought vigorously. We have said how good fortune sometimes helps the bold: Valerius tells of another knight of Julius Caesar named Scaevola, who by chance found himself alone on an island of his enemies, who attacked him bitterly. But he fought so much and so hard that five knights, fighting all day, could hardly do what he did in a short while, and when his darts* failed him he ran at them with his naked sword and did so many feats of arms that the Romans were amazed (they were on the other side of the water, so they could not come to his aid). And it was a hard thing for his enemies to believe that so many blows resulted from one lone knight, and his enemies were ashamed that a single man could withstand so many people, and that despite all their power, he received so few blows against him. And then he was so hard pressed (because he had a lance through his thigh, his face was bruised by a stone, and he was wounded in many places) he threw himself into the sea completely armed. The water he swam in turned red with his blood and that of those he had killed on the shore, whose blood ran down in a great stream. And so he escaped and went to his lord, Julius Caesar, who received him with great honor, and rewarded him generously as he well deserved (Julius Caesar knew how to recognize the good and rewarded them well, so that others would follow their example). So he made him constable and master of large company of knights.

On the subject that fortune sometimes helps the bold knight to escape from great peril and to do many marvels: Valerius tells of another noble Roman knight who had the name Horatius Cocles. Once the Tuscans came to take a bridge against the army of the Romans. This Horatius passed over the bridge and held back the army so that the bridge was broken, and then escaped on his horse into the water safe and sound despite the many lances thrown.

On the valor, boldness, and great courage of knighthood, Valerius tells of a Roman knight who was a marvelous warrior in battles. He was so badly wounded that he could no longer use his hands and believed his life would be brief. So he did as much as he could with his feet to attack one of his enemies, and then, standing on top of him, he seized his nose with his teeth and tore up his whole face!

Valerius tells of a noble prince of Rome named Paulus Crassus, who after fighting valiantly in a battle against Aristonicus, king of Asia, had the misfortune to be captured in battle. Since it was the custom in many places that prisoners taken in battle were held like serfs and given heavy labor, he then realized that he would rather die honorably than live in servitude. Even at Rome they had this custom, especially against those who rebelled against them or broke their treaties with them. So when this noble prince was disarmed by his enemies, he had a stick which he put in the eye of the person who was nearest, and when that person felt the pain, he killed Crassus with his sword. Valerius praised this act saying that Crassus showed Fortune that he was not in her power. Although his body was conquered by her, his courage was still not conquered.

There was another marvelous Roman knight, whom Valerius and many other history writers, such as Varro,* Titus Livius, and others confirm. It seems an impossible to be true, but the authority of these worthy witnesses adds weight to them. There was a noble and mighty knight called Sicinius Dentatus. To speak briefly, he was in 120 victorious battles in his time for the Romans. He had such strength of body and will that it was because of him that a major part of them were won. He brought the spoils of thirty defeated enemies, that is, he won their armor, their shields or cloaks, which was the custom then as a sign of great and complete victory. Eight of those who were despoiled were knights who called him to fight hand-to-hand in front of the two armies. He rescued twenty-four knights from death and was wounded in his chest fourteen times, but he had no wounds in his back. And so, because it was the very noble custom in Rome as I said before (would to God, they would do the same in France which is the flower of all the countries of the world as to nobleness) that when the princes of Rome were victorious in any great conquest they were received with the great honor called a triumph, and the knights who were of higher rank walked nearest the chariot and had their own medals made of jewels, which they wore according to the deeds they had done, and they called them "victors." This valiant and mighty knight Sicinius brought many such victories to Rome. Walking nearest the chariot, he was held in honor many times, but the number of well done deeds grew with the number of victories he had, and the last time he had 312 according to Solinus* and Valerius says 412. When he entered the city he was stared at much more for his amazing deeds than for all the other riches of the triumph itself. And this Sicinius, said Solinus, was the most excellent of the Romans in strength and in boldness.

## Chapter 9 On the third good condition that knights and captains ought to have

It commonly happens that a person who has been instructed in or taught an art or custom, works hard and takes trouble to teach others, and incline them to the same thing; therefore, the sages say, "If you keep company with the good, you will come to resemble them, but if you often see the evil, you will become like them." And so if one desires to be master of an art or a science, it is necessary to associate with the masters and practitioners of whatever one desires to do. For as will be described in the last part of this book, one ought to believe every expert in his own art. On our subject, that is the third condition that the good knight or soldier ought to have, as we discussed in the beginning of this second part, any nobleman in arms ought to honor and emulate the good and noble both in the theory and practice of this science. That I call it "science" could seem to be an error to some, but it seems to me (to speak clearly without quibbling over subtleties), anything which has correct rules of order and measure that ought to be kept can be called science. And there is nothing in the world in which it is more necessary to keep measure and order than military activity, otherwise in battle everything is confusion, as we know from experience. Vegetius wrote his own book called *The Book of the Science and Art of Chivalry* where he speaks of the rules that ought to be kept. And to prove that it is true that there is no rational art where rules are more necessary, he quotes the very noble knight Scipio Africanus, saying, "The greatest shame in the activity of knighthood is to say I don't believe it." Something ought only to be done after such good advice and counsel and for such good reasons that it could not be a problem of believing or not: because there could be no room for doubt in battle. When there is a mistake, it is not amendable once it is committed in the force and violence of battle. This saying is confirmed by the aforementioned Vegetius in the first book of *Chivalry*. In other things, if one errs one can correct the error or fault, but incorrect orders and misconduct in battle can not be rectified because the misdeed is immediately punished. If such a one dies dishonorably, or flees, or falls into slavery, it is fitting if he is captured and treated harshly because such things are more painful than death to the courageous.

And because we have entered into the chapter where we hope to discuss how good soldiers ought to encourage one another to be valiant, and good, and to have the manners and morals [moeurs] they ought (which words are particularly and principally appropriate for the instruction of leaders and captains of armies and battles), let us tell more about the valiant prince Scipio, mentioned above and what he said to his knights. He said that no one ought to fight his enemies, that is, attack them, without just cause. But if the cause is just, they ought to not wait until they are attacked, for in a just cause, right gives greater boldness. And in such a case a man ought to fight securely, but not unless he is forced to fight. But in the case where he is attacked, if he does not defend himself, it is shameful because it would be cowardice and show little confidence in good fortune, which would be bad.

On the subject of good army leaders, Vegetius says that above all else, it is their duty to be wise and well advised in their duties, because it is a heavy responsibility to provide for so many people, that is, to think about what their needs might be. This means governing a large number of people for the will and good order of all, one's own honor, and the benefit of his sovereign. This is why the ancient dukes and princes of battles of old imagined that some of them were of the lineage of the gods so that their subjects and underlings feared them more, and put greater weight on their commands. And such tricks were used in advising their people. As Valerius said, in speaking of the great wisdom, valor, and boldness of the noble prince of battle Sertorius,* who to encourage and inspire his people, pretended that the gods revealed to him what he should do through a white doe which he brought with him to the mountains of Lucitania (which is a part of Spain) and on his other journeys.

And King Minos of Crete did the same. He was a man of the greatest wisdom both in doing justice and in battle, for he subjected and enslaved the Athenians that Theseus, their duke, later freed. This Minos customarily went at the new year to a cavern or cave which in ancient times was consecrated to the god Jupiter, of whom he pretended to be the son, according to the songs of the poets. He said that his father Jupiter gave him the laws and rules which he established. He used this pretense so that they hesitated to break his laws. But these stories are not told so that the good captain or good soldier teaches his people to use evil arts or to pretend to use them, for that would be evil and a bad example. But the wise captain or leader of soldiers could wisely pretend to be greater than he is, or that he had done more than he really did, or to have a good and rational cause for whatever he does, and if he finds any good and just deception, I believe that it is well and wisely done, as will be shown later.

## Chapter 10 On the same subject, with examples

To treat the subject of good exhortations that the good military leader should give his people in as many just forms that he can think of, so that he can give them a greater willingness to do well, to be bold,

and so that they encourage each other, Valerius says that Caius Mar-
cius, consul of Rome, and duke and leader of a great army, once
found himself hard pressed in battle, and greatly feared that the battle
would turn against him and his army. He had foreign soldiers with
him, numbering 300 cohorts (a cohort is 105 men) whom he feared
would not keep faith with him. So to prevent betrayal, seeing that
the situation was urgent and dangerous, he went to them and
exhorted them to do well, and promised them that if he won the
battle due to them he would reward them greatly by making them all
citizens of Rome. This was not a little thing that he promised them,
for it was the greatest honor and benefit that one could give because
of the noble freedoms and liberties which it gave, and it was not
something customarily done for foreigners. These soldiers fought
hard, apparently very joyful at this offer to pay them well. Consequently they suffered greatly since it was a most difficult battle,
and the enemy force was fierce against them, but they won a great
victory. So the consul kept his promise, although it was against the
laws of the city, for no consul ought to do such a thing without the
permission and command of the Senate, that is, the whole council.
But he excused himself for his trespass in front of the Senate, saying
that the immediate danger of battle required a hasty remedy, and he
could not encourage them by any other means except by giving them
a large and unexpected reward. But he had had neither the leisure
nor the space to consider the civil law, which had more need to be
defended than to be observed at this dangerous hour.

On the subject of the wise exhortations of the leader who encourages his people well, Titus Livius, in his first book on the foundation
of Rome, said the Romans had once needed the help of other soldiers
for a battle, and they hired foreign mercenaries. These soldiers who
were neither good nor loyal, considered that the battle was very
doubtful for the Romans. So they left the army and went to the next
mountain so that after the battle they could go over to whichever side
won. When the duke and prince of the army saw this, and saw that
the people were frightened seeing that those who were to help them
were leaving, like a wise leader, he forestalled their fear. He spurred
his horse on immediately and rode through the army saying that it
was by his orders that the captain of these soldiers had all his men
on the summit of the hill, so that they would attack their enemies
from the rear, and that this was the precise job he had given them.

And so this wise and noble leader, by his wisdom and good exhortations, changed their fear into confidence and courage, and he was victorious over his enemies.

## Chapter 11 On the same subject plus examples

On this subject of good exhortations being worth a lot in battle, I can describe three noble knights, one of whom was from Lacedemonia, which is a part of Greece. By his words and his deeds he showed his noble courage. He had found himself *en route* with some soldiers from his country who were going to war, and he went with them. And because he was lame, the others rebuked him asking him what he was going to do. He answered them wisely saying that he went to fight and not to flee. He hoped to bring his strength of arms allied to the constancy of his courage to the battle, or die, and there ashamed, with their whole bodies, if he would earn more glory than they. This good knight said this so that they would compete against each other to strive to fight well in battle. And so it happened: they were so competitive that they brought themselves before their captain to judge who had behaved best in battle, so that he would have a particular honor given him. And because of this challenge to them, they desired to fight so hard that they won a great and difficult victory.

Another Roman knight who was a captain of soldiers had the Romans send a whole company of knights to the help of one of their princes who was fighting in Persia. They came across an army of their men who were returning and who said that the Persians shot so many arrows that the sun could not be seen. This good captain, who saw these men were afraid, answered them sturdily saying "This is good news since we will fight better in the shade." And so, by his bold words and good admonitions he convinced them to return and to fight vigorously.

The other knight was from Greece and was going to the aid of a city with a company of soldiers when he came to a fortress. The citizens who did not dare go outside the walls for fear of their enemies, showed him the high walls and deep ditches of their city. And he answered them this way: "If you have built them for the women, that is good. But if you have built them for the men, it is a shameful and dishonorable thing that you have more faith in the protection of walls and ditches than the greatness of your own strength." And by these wise and good exhortations he gave them heart and boldness to attack their enemies, which they had never dared before. And so they conquered them and broke the siege.

## Chapter 12 Examples of valorous knights

A noble knight of great vigor who had been well trained by Julius Caesar, called Senola, was with Caesar and other knights during the war between Julius Caesar and Pompey. He had been assigned by Caesar to guard a certain pass and a tower against Pompey's army. So Pompey's army decided to attack them so that they would have too much to do and suffer to hold this pass, so the battle was fierce because there were valiant men on both sides. This Senola, bold as a lion, fought so well that it was marvelous, and he had already suffered serious wounds. So he said to his companions in combat: "Forward young knights, my dear friends and companions, break their darts and arrows in your fists and take their arrow heads in your throats, and we shall win, for although we shall die, this fortress will be rescued." In short, such was the great vigor of the deeds and words of this valiant man Senola, that they have to be remembered. For because of his good advice and the example of his deeds, his companions feared nothing and fought marvelously. He climbed the tower and threw the dead off onto the living so that he knocked them down. He cut off the hands of those who gripped the walls to climb them, without ceasing to throw stones. In short, he killed so many that the mound of the dead was as high as the wall, as testify the authentic authors of Roman deeds. And then he fell among the enemy, who ran him through from every side. He struck so many that his sword was greasy with blood, and so dulled from use that it would cut no more. His enemies threw so many darts at him that they were in each other's way. And as Lucan* testifies, he lasted a long time.

Lucan tells us about his marvelous strength and the boldness of his deeds: he was pressed so hard that he could scarcely endure. Among other wounds, he received one in his left eye, but he pulled the arrow out with the eye on it and stepped on it. And when Senola felt that he could not hold out any longer he pretended to regret fighting against the citizens of Rome, and said that they ought to have pity on him since they were of the same blood, and he pleaded with them to be brought

74

to Pompey the Great, to cry for mercy since he preferred to die there. One of them believed him and captured him in good faith. Then Senola struck a great blow which killed him, and so Senola died, one of the best knights who has ever been in the world.

## Chapter 13 On the fourth good condition which valorous military men ought to have

Since the rank of nobility, that is, noblemen, have among the highest and most exalted of honors in this world, it is reasonable that they be adorned with the virtues which are properly called noble as well. Without them, nothing is noble. So Juvenal* says, "Nothing enobles a person except virtue." And Boethius in his *Consolation* proved this saying, that the word "noble" is useless and vain if not illuminated by virtue and generally the ancient authors agree. According to these writings, it is necessary for all who are called noble to be virtuous, that is well-mannered, and that they hate every vice and flee from all unsuitable evils, which are contrary to nobility and that they love and follow all good conditions. Because I have already discussed some of these virtues I will not now. But the fourth of the six good conditions which I have said are necessary to all knights and noblemen at arms, that is, to be true in speech, fealty, and oath, I propose to speak about in this chapter. And because I sometimes burdened myself in others of my books to write about the most blameworthy of the ugly vices, dishonesty – the opposite of truth (which could never be sufficiently reproved by others or by me), I will discuss it only briefly. But about those subjects that concern noblemen, I can say now that it is certainly very evil and dishonorable for them, and which means that some are so defiled that no truth comes out of their mouths, one cannot trust their promises, no more than the promises of the most vile people that exist! And I am speaking of people who call themselves "noble!" Truly such people should carefully consider what nobility is and how little they deserve their rank. They would be confused and ashamed to have so little cause to pride themselves on the nobility of their ancestors, when it is non-existent in themselves.

As for the goodness of truth, I am not worthy to speak sufficiently of it, nor can one say enough. Ah, it is so much praised in Holy Scripture: God is truth, and so calls himself, and all the foundation of our faith and belief is founded on it. All the deeds of the philosophers and their studies are only to attain and search out the truth. And on this Aristotle, in his *Metaphysics* says (which is founded on truth and in which he speaks notably of truth), "All moral philosophy is founded on truth and without it all that we can do in this mortal life is vain and without profit." Alas, that these noble ancients who had no knowledge yet of the divine law, loved death more dearly than to break their law and lie. What shame there is on those who are Christians who for an unimportant thing will lie and perjure themselves as if they did not care!

And we can record many examples of this, like that of a duke of Athens who by misfortune was captured in a battle, despite his side having the victory. His enemy had him in prison and wanted to force him to free himself and his city from a tribute they had to pay to the Athenians. If he would accept, he would also be free, otherwise he would die a martyr's death. But the brave duke answered that he had promised and sworn to protect and maintain their freedoms and jurisdiction without any reduction or loss. So great a harm as losing their possessions was not worth the loss of a man. For they could find as good a prince or better more easily than they could recover their colony, he said. Such was his loyalty to his subjects and faithfulness to the promises he had made before, faced with the death he was going to meet! The noble Roman prince Actilius Regulus, of whom Valerius speaks, is another example of great faithfulness and the keeping of oaths. He was victorious in a battle against a great army of the Carthaginians, and they, to avenge themselves, sent for help to Xantiperus, the king of Lacedemonia, and fought the Romans anew. The turn of Fortune's wheel went against the consul Atilius, and brought him to defeat and he was captured. Five years later, Orosius tells us, the Carthaginians sent their ambassadors to Rome and with them they sent this brave man Atilius. But they made him swear by his faith and his gods that if there was no agreement, he would return to their prison. So they informed the Romans that if they returned the prisoners taken in the first battle, they would return Atilius to them. When the Senate of Rome heard this, they asked the brave Atilius by his faith to advise them and to give his opinion. But the valiant knight counseled them that his person was not worth so great a number of the enemies of the Romans to be released for him alone. He said that exchanging so many of the enemy for him alone was of no benefit to the republic. And so the good man returned to Carthage where he knew terrible tortures awaited him, for he well knew the cruelty of the Carthaginians. But he preferred to die, which he did, than to break his promise.

To explain the customs of Rome: When a prince of Rome had a full victory, and could release Romans who had been captured beforehand by his enemy, when the consul, that is, the prince, returned to the city and was given a "triumph" (as was explained before), these former prisoners were in front of the chariot, with hats of silk on their heads, shaggy, like hats of beaver or felt, as Valerius says. And Titus Livius says that their heads were shaved as a sign that they were free, and no longer slaves. It is really possible to be free and slave at different times, so they said that the silk chaplet signified both slavery and liberty.

Still on the subject of keeping oaths, and the evil that comes with breaking them: when Hannibal, emperor of Carthage, was beaten by the Romans in the second battle, as Titius Livius tells it at the end of the tenth book, the Carthaginians were forced to sue for peace from the Romans, for which purpose they sent ambassadors to Rome. As they told why they had came before the Senate, because they had badly kept the covenants and treaties which they had earlier sworn to, they were addressed thus: "By what gods will you swear peace now, when you have deceived the ones you swore to before and perjured yourselves?" Then one of the messengers, named Hasdrubal, answered saying, "We will swear by the same gods we swore by before when we broke our oaths; you should prefer that since they have avenged themselves so well on the perjurers."

# Chapter 14 On the fifth good condition which a noble soldier ought to have

I said before that the fifth condition that a noble soldier should desire to have is to love honor above all things. And since it is so apparent that it must be so, it is sufficient for me to prove my reasons by examples from the ancients rather than any other arguments.

Themistocles, the noble and valiant knight that I have mentioned elsewhere in this book, so loved and coveted the honor of knighthood that desire for it was like a needle straight to the heart, making him so ardent to acquire honor that he could not rest. He was asked by other knights why he was so busy that he scarcely rested and he answered, "Because the fair and high chivalry of my ancestors and their beautiful victories enflame my courage to follow in their footsteps so I could attain such excellent fame by military activity and practice. But I see myself so far below them that I busy myself and I think unceasingly about it." This good knight was not one of those who thought one little deed sufficient for glory for his whole life, and he performed many excellent deeds.

At the time of Miltiades, Duke of Athens, there was the battle called Marathon* against the Persians. Justin tells of it in the second book of his *History*, which greatly praises his virtues and his great chivalry, for the battle was very heated and fierce. Because of his valor the victory went to Athens, yet it seemed to him but a small thing. Although some maintain that there is no honor except in riches and without them honor is nothing, this opinion is false and wrong, saving their reverence. For let us suppose that honor and reverence were not always awarded today with respect to the virtues as the ancients did, but for riches instead. All the same, no one could tolerate that the virtuous person not be praised and that he not be given the greatest good and most reverence possible for what he had done. Praise and reputation, according to judgment, is more commendable than riches, supposing that person is poor; than to the bad whom one praises to his face but speaks ill behind his back because of his vices.

The ancients gave their honors according to virtue and not for riches, and consequently they went to greater trouble to acquire honor than to acquire treasure. The *History of the Romans* tells that by the will of the whole Roman Senate (that is of all the princes and the Council), the noble Lucius Cyronatus was named dictator, the highest position in Rome, whose story is profitable to hear, Titus Livius says, for those who desire virtue and honor more than riches. He was a very noble man, but very poor; although his valor was well proven, and he was the hope of Rome. The Romans had sent a great army against their enemies, but discovering that they were besieged and were going to be destroyed by their enemies, they made Lucius dictator because they saw that they had insufficient leadership. So they sent to his house outside Rome where he was not ashamed to be found even though it was small and fairly poor, given the height of his position. He immediately went with a good number of his

78

soldiers to the army. And, to be brief, through his wisdom and valor, he defeated those by whom the Roman army was besieged. After they were defeated and the booty taken, he shared the wealth among the soldiers who had been the cause of the defeat, but not those who had been besieged, for he blamed them for their near defeat. And the consul who led them was deposed from his office, for letting them be besieged in their encampment which he had fortified with ditches and a palisade. He said that the man was not worthy of high office and of the dignity of rule because he depended on ditches and a stockade for security rather than strength and virtue, and that he had not been ashamed to keep the Roman army behind closed gates.

In Valerius' third chapter of his fourth book, he tells us of a noble knight who was of very noble ancestry. After many deeds of great strength in many battles against the Volscii and others, he had taken one of their castles, and a much fortified place called Thenolon, for which reason he was nicknamed Thenolanus. He was offered many honors and profitable gifts for his merits that he did not refuse. But he did not care about the many rewards he was offered. According to the customs of Rome to the worthy, he was offered one hundred "days" of land – that is, as much as a plow could prepare in 100 days; also ten prisoners that he could choose from among the captured, ten richly adorned and armed horses, ten oxen, and as much silver as he could carry. But he accepted none of it except for one prisoner who had been his host and had been friendly to him. To pay him back the same way, he gave him his freedom and a war horse, for which virtue, Valerius said, one could not know which gave him greater honor, that is, for what he chose or what he refused; to take so little or refuse so much.

## Chapter 15 On the same subject and how in the old days one honored the chivalrous according to their merits

Continuing the subject of how the ancients preferred honors to riches as all who are noble should do, Valerius speaks of Scipio Africanus (minor, for the two Scipios so nicknamed were both such valiant men that there was hardly any difference between them, for both conquered Africa by great labor and many battles, but the first conquered it for the Romans, the second recaptured it with great difficulty, after they had rebelled). This Scipio destroyed the city of Carthage as well as the city of Ammance, brought war against the Gauls (now called the French), and against the Lombards, and was victorious over them. After these victories, he would share the honors and booty with his knights. Then he ordered according to custom that everyone report to the chief prince of the battle the valiant deeds that each knight had done, for they had men, that we could call "heralds," who were responsible for this, and they took care that each be rewarded or punished according to what they deserved. One knight, according to the others, fought better, and he was given a certain gold medal which he was ordered to wear on his shoulder, like those who showed similar accomplishments. These were called "armilles." Scipio then inquired about the knight to see if he had done other great deeds or if it had just happened that way this time. So he discovered that this was his first great deed of war, but that he seemed to be of good will. To test him further, Scipio called him into his presence and offered him a lot of gold coins, like those we call "florins," and told him "It is possible to pay for your deed in riches and not in honor." When the knight who was offered the gold heard this he was saddened and shamed and he threw the gold at the feet of Scipio. So he was asked if he would prefer gold or honor more as a reward for valor and he said he preferred honor. Then Scipio praised him even more, but to test his constancy and his perseverance in arms, he gave him an insignia of silver, which was made of gold in similar cases, and told him that he would one day acquire a golden one if he deserved it. And Scipio showed that honor should not be given for one good deed alone, which could come from fortune, but was given for being persevering in good works.

## Chapter 16 How lechery and pleasure are often the cause of turning one away from achieving honor and valor

In order to acquire honor by arms as is discussed in this part of the book, one ought to pursue everything that is suitable and flee and avoid everything which can impede and detract from one's intention. But I find in the writings that among the other vices, pleasures and lechery are the ones that most destroy the deeds of those who have begun and even persevered for a long time in valor and honor. Notwithstanding that I spoke already to princes in this treatise about the avoidance of pleasures, I am moved to give some examples. The army of Antiochus,* the great king of Persia and Asia, had beaten the Romans and frightened them very often. And after many victories in Greece, they went to Chalcidia where they entertained themselves with pleasures, lechery, and gambling. They spent the whole winter there, and became soft. As Macrobius tells us, when Antiochus wanted to fight against the Romans again, he took Hannibal with him to look at the strength and nobility of his army. He asked Hannibal if there were enough for the Romans. Hannibal answered that "Yes, despite their great greed!" But this was not the answer Antiochus wanted, because he wanted to know if he had enough power to defeat the Romans. So Hannibal, who had tested their virtue many times, saw that Antiochus' knights were too spoiled and too full of pomp, so he answered that the riches that he saw in this army would have to content the Romans, even though they were very greedy people. So it happened, despite the fact that the histories say that Antiochus was marvelously rich and had so much power that he sent 109 elephants into battle against the Romans, each one carrying a tower made of wood which was filled with soldiers, and his army covered mountains and valleys – nonetheless they were defeated by the Romans.

On this subject, that pleasure and too much ease soften and weaken the will, the authors tell us that the city of Voulques was rich and well-governed. It was the capital of the land of Accrusia, but its enormous riches inclined it to pleasure and lechery for which reason the vices dominated it, and it declined by becoming so soft in defense and it was subjugated by slaves. And it is important to note that from one vice, others may follow, which is something the good knight should guard against, since vice may lead to loss of honor in princes and in others.

## Chapter 17 How the ancients rewarded the good deeds of the good according to their merits, and the honors that they gave them

To return to our first subject, how the virtuous soldier ought to prefer honor to other things, we have proven this by examples of noble ancients who wanted to be valorous and how they were rewarded for their good deeds. So we will give another example of how remuneration should be given without favoritism.

Valerius tells that when a noble man named Calpurnius Piso was made consul and prince of a great army, he defeated Sicily by great battles and came to give gifts to his soldiers according to the customs of the Romans, each one according to his merit. He had a son who was a most valiant knight and for the good he had done in battle those who gave the reports judged that a gold crown was the honor he best deserved. But his father debated for a long time and decided that it was deserved more by others. By the judgment of all, despite the opinion of his father, the crown was awarded to him by the common voice, and, I believe he preferred this honor over a pile of gold. In those days, the honor was given to them according to their worth and it was very much desired. Valerius says that when someone's military deed surpassed the others in excellence of courage, boldness and strength the Romans made a noble image and seated it in an honorable and prominent place dedicated to this use and wrote his name and details of what he had done below it. And thus they had a memorial to them so that they would be an example to others, so that one made great effort to be honored this way. And they treated clerks likewise: if there was a philosopher or a notable man, or woman, like the wise Sibyl, who surpassed others in wisdom or in learning; or an artisan made images with such skill that they seemed alive, or an artisan of any craft did excellent work, they were honored likewise. And so, as you see, they desired glory and honor, these noble ancients, with which desire Valerius agrees, saying that the virtuous should desire honor, glory, and reverence. This is shown by the virtuous Scipio Africanus who put the image of Ennius the poet among the statues of his ancestors because he honored them in his writings.

And so that no one can contradict this opinion, arguing that glory and honor should not be desired in this world, but despised, Valerius shows how those who in their books claim to despise glory, desire and want it just as much as others do. And, he says, glory is certainly not despised by those who teach this idea, for they carefully put their names on the volumes and books which they write. They praise people who do not care about glory, but they still want to acquire glory; perpetuating their names by writing them on their books. And so we conclude this chapter, saying that the good and noble ought to and can desire glory, despite the fact that Boethius argues in his third book, not to quest too ardently for glory in this world, and not at all in the spiritual life. But for those who live morally in the active life, to desire glory in a just cause is not a vice.

## Chapter 18 Which speaks of the sixth condition which noble soldiers ought to have

The sixth condition which the good soldier ought to fulfil, as I said before, is that he be wise, well-advised, and clever in all the things which pertain to arms and deeds of chivalry. To show this, we will give examples of crafty deeds of noble knights who made great conquests and did great things in their time, to be remembered both so that they may be used and so as not to be deceived by them if they are used against us. These are described by the authors and especially Valerius who calls such subtleties used to conquer and destroy the enemy "strategems."

The first example is that of Philostratus who was Duke of Athens. He was very subtle and crafty in everything, the histories tell us, but especially in war, as can be seen in the story of a Greek city called Megara. In the past, they had fought a war with Athens, which they continued while feigning peace. At the time of Philostratus, the Megarians thought they were about to avenge themselves on Athens, because they had not forgotten the grief and damage that had been done to them. Knowing of the Athenian custom of traveling to the island of Euletre where the ladies of Athens went on pilgrimage one day each year, they hoped to surprise them with their naval ships full of soldiers when they dropped their guard. Philostratus, duke of Athens was warned of this and ordered the women to go as they were accustomed. They should dress in their finest and have their feasts more than ever, so that the Megarians would not realize they had been warned. So he took soldiers with him and went to the island, and prepared an ambush. And as soon as the Megarians came, they attacked and killed them all. And then Philostratus loaded their ships with a large group of women in their finest clothing and turned the ships towards Megara so that they believed their ships returned with the women and their booty. And so it happened, for they recognized their ships and their ensigns. In their joy, everyone came to the port, whereupon they were all killed. Soon after, the city was captured.

Darius (who was chosen king of the Persians and the Medes by the neighing of his horse) assembled 600,000 men, as Justin tells us, to destroy the city of Athens and the countryside around it. The Athenians sent messengers to Lacedemonia and elsewhere for help, but it was too slow in coming. Miltiades, who was Duke of Athens then, found he had only 10,000 of his own men and no foreign mercenaries at all. Yet this valiant man had more trust in attacking his enemies immediately than in waiting for the help to come, despite many of his own men being against it. So he attacked them more quickly than they ever thought he would, and they did not have time to prepare, and they scattered and were in disarray, so in this battle 10,000 defeated 600,000 Persians.

Valerius says that Hannibal, Emperor of Carthage, hated the noble Roman prince Fabius Maximus the most because he had done him many injuries in battle and resisted his army by force. Titus Livius also said that this was the Roman prince that Hannibal hated the most. Fabius Maximus was dictator, which was the highest office at Rome, and leader of a great army. So Hannibal thought of a trick to destroy Fabius: he destroyed all the fields of Italy, putting all the flat country to the torch, except the lands and manors that belonged to the dictator Fabius, so that the Romans would suspect him of some alliance. Then he did even more: He found a way to send secret letters to Rome which came to the hands of the council addressed to Fabius by Hannibal, who was not at the time in the city. The letters made it appear that there was familiarity and promises between them, which was Hannibal's invention. Had the Romans not believed in the loyalty of Fabius and the malice and cleverness of Hannibal, he might have succeeded in his intention.

## Chapter 19 Of wise tricks in arms that the knights ought to use

Every prince and knight should be well-advised and well-informed about the conditions, the sense, and the malice of his adversary, and inquire if he is accustomed to using trickery and subterfuge. The examples that follow will show that it appears he is given cause to guard himself from the malicious, for as a sage says, "Keep yourself from those who conduct themselves with trickery, and the more they flatter you, the more you should be on your guard." For the malicious

84

are like a cat, that waits to act. When it sees the mouse that it wants to attack and eat up, it wags its tail in friendship. Just so, the deceiver also sits and waits and when the time comes, he smiles at those he wants to deceive, and then all at once he attacks him.

It is written that there was once a king of a part of Greece who was amazingly deceitful and tricky. He hated and envied the Romans the most, but he never dared to invade them openly because of their great strength, so he used trickery. He pretended to be their ally because of their great reputation. And he knew that nothing will so undermine and surprise human hearts as handsome gifts, no matter who gives it. So he often sent gifts accompanied by very amiable words to the principal councillors of Rome, and because of this he knew about their schemes, which he found ways to undermine in many ways. But when the Romans wanted to go after him, the good friends that he had made in Rome always supported him and appeased them. And he kept safe this way for a long time so he was not punished. Moreover, this fraud pretended that he had a great desire to go to Rome to see the magnificence of the city, and he offered the princes to do anything he could in their service. He knew so well how to behave that he was well-received and honored and, while he was there, presented himself to be a friend to them as much as he could. But when they came to him to honor him, he encouraged conflict among them and pretended to each that what he said was for their good and to keep it secret; in this way he caused great hatred among them.

And when he saw what he had accomplished, and he had studied well the ways and laws of the place, he left, and as he went out of the gates of Rome, he said, loud enough for many to hear "Rome is strong, but for those who have enough wealth, Rome is weak." This example is given so as to show that one ought to be careful of a fraudulent person who at the same time gives generously, because, as Ovid said, even the gods can be appeased by gifts.

Tarquin,* the king of Rome, laid siege for a long time to the city of Galbine and could not capture it, so his son advised him to use trickery. He cut himself and then went to the city of Galbine saying that the king his father had beaten and wronged him and he wanted to avenge himself if he could. He wanted to be their friend if it pleased them, and he pleaded to be allowed into their city. Those that believed what he said received him joyfully and he complained bitterly about his father. He knew how to flatter them so that they made him master of the city and ruler of all. When he became ruler, he sent a message to his father saying "Trickery overcomes force." The father said nothing but seemed pensive, and went to a garden with the messenger. The garden was filled with poppies, so then he took a knife and cut off the heads of the tallest flowers, but said nothing. The messenger asked if the king wanted to send message to his son. He said that he would send no word. The messenger reported to the son that the king had said nothing but that he seemed sad as he cut off the heads of the tallest poppies. The son understood his "words" well. He found a way to claim that all the most important people of the city were conspiring against him, and wanted to deliver the city over to his father. And so he cut off their heads. And when there were no leaders to contradict him, he turned the city over to his father. This story is told by many authors, especially Titus Livius.

Also in the time that Rome was captured by the Gauls (now called the French), they were besieging the Capitol which could only be captured by starving them out. But the Romans tricked them by undermining their hopes. They took the supplies they had – great platters of meat and fine bread and all kinds of foodstuffs – and threw them over the walls as rubbish. When the Gauls saw this they were discouraged and believed that if they could waste such a quantity of supplies then they must have plenty. So they sued for peace.

Valerius says that before he fought the Romans in the long fierce battle of Cannae, Hannibal tried to weaken the Romans by three tricks. First, he saw to it that he had the sun and dust at his back, for there was a strong wind. Secondly, he commanded that when the battle began, a part of his men should pretend to flee, and when they did, the Romans who followed them were ambushed by hidden soldiers, who killed them all. Third, he commanded that a part of his men should surrender early in battle. They were disarmed and were sent back behind the lines. But they had hidden short, very sharp swords on their bodies and when the Romans were fighting they attacked them from the rear and wounded the soldiers. And so Valerius says, the force of Rome was vanquished by the cleverness of Africa.

## Chapter 20 More examples of wise trickery in arms

Pericles, who was duke of Athens, was driven by the Peloponnese into an enclosed valley between high and horrible mountains. The valley had only two exits and when he saw himself thus enclosed he immediately went to one of the exits and made a large and deep ditch apparently so that his enemies could not come after him by this route. He brought his people to the other exit seemingly so that they could fight their way out. His enemies did not believe that he wanted or even could escape from one end because of the ditch, so they all waited at the other exit. Then Pericles immediately put wooden bridges that he had prepared over the ditch and his army went safely out this way.

The Roman army also had to pass by the Latin forest in order to fight against the people of Voieux. When these people realized this they went to the same forest, and cut almost all the trees so that they would easily fall, and prepared everything for an ambush. As soon as the Roman army entered the forest, the Voieux came out from everywhere, knocking the trees down onto the Romans, and killed the whole army this way.

Alexander, king of Pyrrha was fighting a war against the Eleriens, so he devised this trick: he had them bring together a great mound of clothing like the Eleriens wore on their armor, and dressed his people in them, and when he knew the enemy was near by he put his men dressed thus to set fire to the buildings in his own country. The Eleriens saw this and believed that it was their own men and they wanted to join them through a narrow pass. Alexander ambushed them as they went through and everyone was killed or captured.

Once, those that fought against a people called Hericees captured a spy, so they killed him and dressed one of their men of the same height in his clothes. He was sent up on a hill where they could see him and he signaled them to come forward, and they did, thinking he was the spy they had sent. In this manner they surprised the enemy in ambush and they were all massacred and killed.

There was also Lentulus, who, needing soldiers, hired a number of Macedonians as mercenaries. When Lentulus and his whole army were near the enemy, the Macedonians, who believed they would be in the worst of the battle, left the army and went over to the enemy to fight for them. So Lentulus immediately sent his army forward, and followed them in battle order. When the enemy saw this, they believed that the Macedonians who were in front had been ordered to begin the battle and they fought hard against them. The Macedonians who saw they were not welcomed by them, were forced to fight, so they fought as hard as they could against those they wanted to give themselves up to, and Lentulus was victorious.

## Chapter 21 On the same subject

Aulius Nobileus was once so oppressed by his enemies, the Samites, that it was necessary for him to fight them. Against their very large army, he had only few people and they were very much afraid. Aulius could see the fear of his army so he used a ruse. He told his people that he had bribed a large part of the enemy to fight for him once the battle began. To make his story believable, he borrowed all the gold his men had in order to pay the legion that he said he had bribed (a legion numbered 6666). This gave them the confidence to fight with such boldness that they defeated their enemies.

Epaminondas, ruler of Thebes, had to fight against the Lacedemonians so he wanted to give confidence and strength to his soldiers. So he assembled them all in place and told them that he knew for truth that if the Lacedemonians won they would deliberately kill the men, women and children of Thebes, which so angered the Thebans that they fought like wildmen and defeated their enemy.

Now on the subject that all captains and leaders of armies should be wise and well advised in deed and in word, the following examples are offered: when Scipio Africanus Minor brought his army by sea to Africa, as he came off the ship he fell flat, which frightened his men who thought it was an evil omen. When the wise prince saw that his knights and people were pensive and worried, he advised them to put their hearts at rest. Getting to his feet he said joyfully, "This is an omen of possession. Now let us go, my knights, for I have already 'seized' Africa!" This comforted them greatly and so it happened as he said.

Sertorius was going with a large army of Romans against another people that was an enemy of Rome. Suddenly there appeared a marvelous sign: all the shields of the men and the chests of the horses seemed covered with blood. Sertorius, like a wise leader, saw that his people were afraid and said immediately, "No doubt we will have the victory over our enemies this time, because it is our shields and our horses that are most often covered with the blood of enemies!"

Also, to speak of well-advised people who removed by wise ruse the suspicions that one might have of them, Valerius said that when

88

Hannibal was emperor of Africa and Carthage, he fled for refuge to the king of Crete for fear of the Romans, after his good fortune had turned to bad. He noticed that his great victories caused envy and the fear that he might have plans against them so he decided on a ruse to give them security so that he did not have to worry about them asking for the few goods he had left. He took some chests and filled them with lead, as though it was his treasury – his jewels and dishes – and put them in the temple of Diana* as if it would be the only place where his fortune could be safe. This convinced the Cretans and kept them from having suspicions about his motives there.

And by these stories one can clearly see that subtle tricks are sometimes good and profitable.

Here ends the second part of this book.

# On the Common People

Here begins the third part of this book, which is addressed to the universal people.

## Chapter 1 The first chapter discusses how the estates must unite and come together

In the first part of this book concerning the instruction of princes, we depicted the aforementioned prince or princes as the head of the body politic, as planned before. Thereafter followed the second part, on the education of nobles and knights, which are the arms and the hands. In this part, with God's help, let us continue with what we can pluck from the authorities on this subject of the life of the body of the aforementioned polity, which means the whole of the people in common, described as the belly, legs, and feet, so that the whole be formed and joined in one whole living body, perfect and healthy. For just as the human body is not whole, but defective and deformed when it lacks any of its members, so the body politic cannot be perfect, whole, nor healthy if all the estates of which we speak are not well joined and united together. Thus, they can help and aid each other, each exercising the office which it has to, which diverse offices ought to serve only for the conservation of the whole community, just as the members of a human body aid to guide and nourish the whole body. And in so far as one of them fails, the whole feels it and is deprived by it.

Thus it is appropriate to discuss the way the final parts of the body should be maintained in health and in well-being, for it seems to me that they are the support and have the burden of all the rest of the body, thus they need the strength and the power to carry the weight of the other parts. This is why, just as we said earlier, the good prince must love his subjects and his people, and we spoke of the office of nobles which is established to guard and defend the people.

It is suitable to speak of the love, reverence, and obedience that his people should have for the prince. So let us say to all universally: all the estates owe the prince the same love, reverence, and obedience. But after I have said something about the increase of virtue in their life and manner of living, perhaps I will discuss the three ways the different classes ought to express the generalized principle. And because sometimes there are complaints among the three different estates – princes, knights, and people – because it seems to each of them that the other two do not do their duty in their offices, which can cause discord among them, a most prejudicial situation, here is a moral tale told as a fable:

> Once upon a time there was great disagreement between the belly of a human body and its limbs. The belly complained loudly about the limbs and said that they thought badly of it and that they did not take care of it and feed as well as they should. On the other hand, the limbs complained loudly about the belly and said they were all exhausted from work, and yet despite all their labor, coming and going and working, the belly wanted to have everything and was never satisfied. The limbs then decided that they would no longer suffer such pain and labor, since nothing they did satisfied the belly. So they would stop their work and let the belly get along as best it might. The limbs stopped their work and the belly was no longer nourished. So it began to get thinner, and the limbs began to fail and weaken, and so, to spite one another, the whole body died.

Likewise, when a prince requires more than a people can bear, then the people complain against their prince and rebel by disobedience. In such discord, they all perish together. And thus I conclude that agreement preserves the whole body politic. And so attests Sallust, "in concord, little things increase, and by discord, great things decrease."

## Chapter 2 On the differences between the several peoples

Although the writing of books and especially those on manners and instruction must be general and relate to the inhabitants of all countries (since books are carried to many places and regions), because we reside in France we will restrict our words and teaching to the French people, although these words and instruction would seem to generally serve as a good example in all other regions where good and correct understanding is desired.

Throughout the whole world, lands which are governed by humans are subject to different institutions according to the ancient customs of places. Some are governed by elected emperors, others by hereditary kings, and so on. Also there are cities and countries which are self governed and are ruled by princes which they choose among themselves. Often these make their choice more by will than by reason. And sometimes, having chosen them by caprice, they seem to depose them the same way. Such government is not beneficial where it is the custom, as in Italy in many places.

Other cities are governed by certain families in the city that they call nobles, and they will allow no one not of their lineage to enter their counsels nor their discussions; this they do in Venice which has been governed thus since its foundation, which was very ancient. Others are governed by their elders who are called "aldermen." And in some places, the common people govern and every year a number of persons are installed from each trade. I believe that such governance is not profitable at all for the republic and also it does not last very long once begun, nor is there peace in and around it, and for good reason. But I will not say more for reasons of brevity. Such was the government of Bologna. I would have too much to do to speak of each people separately, but when it comes to choosing the most suitable institution to govern the polity and the community of people, Aristotle says in Book III of the *Politics*, that the polity of one is best, that is, governance and rule by one. Rule by a few is still good, he says, but rule by the many is too large to be good, because of the diversity of opinions and desires.

On our subject, I consider the people of France very happy. From its foundation by the descendants of the Trojans, it has been governed, not by foreign princes, but by its own from heir to heir, as the ancient chronicles and histories tell. This rule by noble French princes has become natural to the people. And for this reason and the grace of God, of all the countries and kingdoms of the world, the people of France has the most natural and the best love and obedience for their prince, which is a singular and very special virtue and praiseworthy of them and they deserve great merit.

## Chapter 3 The obedience to the prince that a people ought to have

It pleases the good to have one's merits be praised, although to be praised scarcely matters to those who are wise. As I have said before, no matter what anyone said to diminish their worth, it causes them to be pleased and delight more in goodness. For just as prudent persons who are curious about their health would like the advice of doctors, even though they have no symptoms of illness, but so they may live in health, it pleases them to have a regimen to preserve their health. Likewise, we will comfort the loyal people of France in order to preserve them in the good and faithful love that they are accustomed to and always have for their very noble, venerable, and above all, praiseworthy and redoubtable princes. And so that they understand and know that by doing so, they act as virtuous and good people, this will be demonstrated here by quotations on the subject from Holy Scripture and other examples.

The Holy Scriptures in many places advise subjects to render themselves humble subjects and to be readily obedient to their lords and rulers. So St. Paul* says in the thirteenth chapter of the Epistle to the Romans: "All living creatures ought to be subject to powerful rulers, for those powers that princes have are commanded by God. And he who resists their power, he is recalcitrant or rebellious against the command of God."

And this same St. Paul, in chapter 3 of the Epistle to Titus, counsels the common people to hold themselves subject to princes and high powers. And this adage is given by St. Peter* in his first epistle, chapter 2, where he says, "Be subject to your lords in fearful dread." But, so that no one can excuse oneself by saying that this only applies to princes that are good, St. Peter declares plainly, "Suppose that the princes were bad," he says, "then subject yourself for the love of God, and especially to the king as most excellent and to the leaders [ducz] sent by God for the punishment of evildoers and for the glory of the good and of their good deeds."

And for those who may complain about the tribute and taxes that it is suitable to pay to princes, they are to understand that it is a thing permitted and accepted by God. And so Holy Scripture gives an example to demonstrate how subjects ought not to refuse to pay that which is commanded. In chapter 22 of his gospel, Saint Matthew* tells how the Pharisees asked Our Lord* if they must pay taxes to Caesar the emperor, to which Our Lord answered, saying "Give to Caesar that which is Caesar's and to God that which is His," which means that taxes are due to the prince. In the seventeenth chapter of his gospel, Saint Matthew also tells how Our Lord sent St. Peter to the river and told him to look in the mouth of the first fish which he caught and he would find a coin. And He told him to take this coin to those who collected the taxes of the emperor in payment for the two of them. Thus, our Lord himself gave an example of being subject in deed and in word to revere and obey lords and princes. On this point of loyalty towards the prince, I believe that God has saved the people of France from many perils, because of their goodness and merit.

All subjects ought accordingly to be loyal towards their prince, and evil comes from doing the opposite. Therefore let us return to Valerius and other authors on this subject. In chapter 8, book 6, Valerius tells of the loyalty which a person named Papinion had towards his lord. He knew that his lord was spied on by those who hated him to death and he could not escape if he were found. And so, in order to save him, he took his lord's robe and his ring, and wrapped him in his own and secretly took him out of the palace and stayed there in his place. When his enemies came, he let them kill him in order to save his lord and master. Valerius said that although the narration of this deed was brief, as a subject for praise, it is not.

On the topic of the evils that come to a people that rebels against the prince, so that one can guard against it, book 18 of the book of Trogus Pompeius tells how the people of a Greek city rebelled so much against their lord that they wanted to kill him, and in fact did kill his wife and children and all his lineage. Nonetheless there is always one person who is less evil than the rest. One of the citizens named Strato when he found his lord hidden in fear, did not want to kill him but had pity on him and wanted to keep him from death. He hid him to save him and the people believed he had fled. And when the people had done this, they wanted to choose one of themselves to be king. But because they were divided on who it should be, they decided that they assemble in a field the next day before sunrise, and the first to see the sun rise would be their king. Strato, who had saved the king from death, took counsel with him that night about how he could see the sun first in order to be king. His lord, who wanted to return the courtesy for the life that he had saved, advised him that when everyone looked to the east, Strato should look to the west towards the city. So they were all together, looking towards the rising sun, when Strato, who was looking in the opposite direction, saw the rays of the sun hit the top of a high tower. And so he showed it to the others who could not see it yet. Then everyone was much amazed and asked him who had given him the advice, and he told them how he had saved his lord, and everything.

A long time after, in the time when Alexander the Great reigned, the treason of this people to its lord was spoken of. And Alexander wanted to avenge the king and went to attack the city and take it by force and punish them severely. Because the king that he had saved was dead, he confirmed Strato in his kingdom and ordered that his children would reign after him because of the kindness he had done his lord.

# Chapter 4 Here we begin to discuss the third estate of the people, and first, clerics studying the branches of knowledge

In the community of people are found three estates, which means, especially in the city of Paris and other cities, the clergy, the burghers and merchants, and the common people, such as artisans and laborers. Now it is suitable to consider the things to say that are beneficial as examples of good living for each of the distinct estates since they are different. And because the clerical class is high, noble, and worthy of honor amongst the others, I will address it first, that is, the students, whether at the University of Paris or elsewhere.

Oh well advised, oh happy people! I speak to you, the disciples of the study of wisdom, who, by the grace of God and good fortune or nature apply yourselves to seek out the heights of the clear rejoicing star, that is, knowledge, do take diligently from this treasure, drink from this clear and healthy fountain. Fill yourself from this pleasant repast, which can so benefit and elevate you! For what is more worthy for a person than knowledge and the highest learning? Certainly, you who desire it and employ yourself with it, you have chosen the glorious life! For by it, you can understand the choice of virtue and the avoidance of vice as it counsels the one and forbids the other.

There is nothing more perfect than the truth and clarity of things which knowledge demonstrates how to know and understand. There is no treasure of the goods of fortune that he who has tasted of the highest knowledge would exchange for a drop of the dregs of wisdom. And truly, no matter what others say, I dare say there is no treasure the like of understanding. Who would not undertake any labor, you champions of wisdom, to acquire it? For if you have it and use it well, you are noble, you are rich, you are all perfect! And this is plain in the teachings of the philosophers, who teach and instruct the way to come through wisdom to the treasure of pure and perfect sufficiency.

The very worthy philosopher Cleanthes,* having already experienced the true desire to taste wisdom, had so much love for it that because he was too poor to buy books or even something to live on, he drew water all night for the needs of students in order to have enough to live on. By day, he listened to the study and the lessons of Chryssipus, who was a very fine philosopher, so that his learning would be complete. Thus by industry and long patience he became a very noble man, who was worthy of the highest praise as much for the constancy of his labor as the knowledge he acquired. Thus, in a letter, Seneca said that Cleanthes, by the labor he had undertaken, helped himself to come to the perfection of knowledge.

On the subject of the love of knowledge and the diligence and care needed to learn, in order to have the great good that comes to those who acquire it, we will tell a little of other philosophers to whet the appetite of those who study.

The philosopher Plato loved knowledge so much that by the hard work of acquiring it, he filled himself with wisdom and learning. This Plato was Aristotle's teacher and lived during the time of Socrates the philosopher. He benefited so much from learning that because of the nobility of his mind he was reputed to be the wisest of all mortal men. And he showed that he was fond of knowledge, for he went everywhere looking for books, even to Italy. About this, Valerius says that his great diligence and desire for learning took him to consult books everywhere, and so, by him, knowledge was expanded and dispersed around the world.

This eminent man died at the age of eighty-one. His death showed the love he had for all kinds of books, for found near him were the books of a woman poet, named Sappho,* who wrote about love in joyous and graceful verses, so Orosius says. And so, perhaps he looked at them to take pleasure in her pleasant poems.

Valerius' book tells of the philosopher Democritus,* who, according to what Aristotle says in the first book of *On Generation and Corruption*, was concerned about everything, that is, that he wanted to talk and debate about everything that was said. Therefore, Aristotle recommended his natural philosophy and his opinions in many places. He is praised and recommended so much by Valerius because, first, he despised riches, which many times are an impediment to the acquisition of philosophy, and also he tells how Democritus was able to abandon his riches, which were so great that his father could give food to Xerxes'* entire army. Nonetheless, so that he could retire to study, he threw aside the concerns and occupations that come to those with wealth; he distributed all that he had and retained scarcely what he needed to live on.

Secondly, Valerius recommends him because he did not seek worldly honors, which are an impediment to the conquest of wisdom. And because he lived for a long time in Athens, employing all his time in educating himself, and he lived unknown in the city. As he testifies in one of his volumes, he chose the solitary life to be outside the tumult that impedes thought. So it appears that he had a great desire for wisdom, for he avoided with all his power anything which could hinder his acquisition of it.

On the subject of the love of knowledge and study, Valerius says of the philosopher Carneades,* that he was the upright, hardworking knight of wisdom, because, for eighty years he lived as a philosopher. So amazing was his concentration on works of learning that he often forgot to take his meal at table. He was so abstracted that his loyal servant, Meleisa, would put his food in his hand. This philosopher cared for nothing in the world but virtue.

I could speak of other noble philosophers and seekers of wisdom, but will not, for the sake of brevity. I tell the above stories to bring them to the memory of good students so that they see that books of such topics can teach them knowledge in order that they may increase in goodness and virtue. For there is no doubt that the sciences perfect the habits. If people are so perverse that it suffices them that others think that they know the sciences, and they do not use their wisdom for themselves, but only teach it to others, then they resemble people who die of hunger with food near them. And no doubt, such people are more to blame when they are mistaken than are others.

## Chapter 5 More on the same subject

Because it is an important subject and appropriate to know, and because not everyone has the book by Valerius to study at his pleasure the subjects of which he speaks, it pleases me to speak about study.

As I said before, the student ought to have great diligence in order to acquire wisdom. Valerius teaches how one ought to have moderate diligence and not be too excessive in this exercise. He says that Scaevola, who was an excellent jurist and expert in common law in Rome and who composed many laws, after his arduous work and study, took recreation in a variety of games. And Valerius explained and approved of it, saying that the nature of things does not allow a person to work continually, but that it is necessary to rest and stay sometimes at leisure. Leisure does not mean to do nothing physical, but means any joyful work or sport that will refresh his understanding, because the sensitive qualities of the soul become weak from long attention to study, and they would not be refreshed by complete cessation of all activity. If they give themselves no recreation, those whose work is study become melancholy because the mind is over-worked, and if they go to sleep they will suffer from bad dreams. And so the remedy for such labor is to rejoice the spirit in games and play. Just as rich food pleases us more when alternated with plain food, so the work of study is best nourished when one sometimes plays, and so Cato* says, "vary your work with diversions." In Book 4 of *Ethics*, Aristotle says "one should exercise the virtue of temperance and moderation in work and play;" to which Seneca, in his book *On Tranquility of Mind*, adds "fertile fields are soon exhausted by continual and uninterrupted cultivation." So continual mental work destroys the strength and leads to frenzy, and so nature gives humans an inclination to play and relax from time to time. It is for this reason that there are laws establishing certain holidays so that people come together in public to bring joy and a cessation of work. On this, it is said of Socrates, from whom no part of wisdom was hidden, that he

was not ashamed when Alcibiades* mocked him for playing with
little children, because it was an account of this recreation that his
understanding was clearer and more lively at study. This is why in
his old age he learned to play the harp.

## Chapter 6 On the second estate of people, that is, the burghers and merchants

I said before that the second rank of people is composed of the
burghers and merchants of the cities. Burghers are those who are
from old city families and have a surname and an ancient coat of
arms. They are the principal dwellers and inhabitants of cities, and
they inherit the houses and manors on which they live. Books refer
to them as "citizens." Such people ought to be honorable, wise, and
of good appearance, dressed in honest clothing without disguise or
affectation. They must have true integrity and be people of worth
and discretion, and it is the estate of good and beneficial citizens. In
some places, they call the more ancient families noble, when they
have been people of worthy estate and reputation for a long time.
And so, in all places, one ought to praise good burghers and citizens
of cities. It is a very good and honorable thing when there is a notable
bourgeoisie in a city. It is a great honor to the country and a great
treasure to the prince.

These people ought to be concerned with the situation and needs
of the cities of which they are a part. They are to ensure that everything concerning commerce and the situation of the population is
well governed. For humble people do not commonly have great prudence in words or even in deeds that concern politics and so they
should not meddle in the ordinances established by princes. Burghers
and the wealthy must take care that the common people are not hurt,
so that they have no reason to conspire against the prince or his
council. The reason is that these conspiracies and plots by the
common people always come back to hurt those that have something
to lose. It always was and always will be that the end result is not at
all beneficial to them, but evil and detrimental. And so, if there is a
case sometime when the common people seem to be aggrieved by
some burden, the merchants ought to assemble and from among
them choose the wisest and most discreet in action and in speech,
and go before the prince or the council, and bring their claims for

them in humility and state their case meekly for them, and not allow them to do anything, for that leads to the destruction of cities and of countries.

So, to the extent of their power, they should quiet the complaints of the people because of the evil that could come to all. They must restrain themselves this way, as well as others. And if sometimes the laws of princes and their council seem to them to appear, according to their judgment, to be wrong, they must not interpret this as in bad faith, and there may be danger in foolishly complaining, but they ought to assume that they have good intentions in what they do, although the cause might not be apparent. It is wisdom to learn when to hold one's tongue, said Valerius, citing Socrates, the most noble and praiseworthy philosopher. Once he was in a place where many complained of the laws of princes, and one of them asked him why he alone said nothing when the others spoke. "Because," said he, "I have sometimes repented of speaking but never of holding my tongue."

It is a noble thing to keep from speaking, from which evil can come and no benefit and it is a proof of wisdom when someone does it. Likewise, wise Cato said, "the first virtue is to hold one's tongue." For one is close to God who by the teaching of reason knows to keep quiet. And in the fifth book of the last work, Seneca said that "he who would be one of the disciples of Pythagoras must be silent for five years, because it is necessary to know what to say before speaking."

## Chapter 7 How the wise burghers ought to counsel the simple* people in what they should do

As was said before, the wise should teach the simple and the ignorant to keep quiet about those things which are not their domain and from which great danger can come and no benefit. And as testimony to this, it is written in chapter 22 of the book of Exodus that the law forbids such complaints and says also "you will not complain about great rulers nor curse the princes of the people." And Solomon confirms this in the tenth chapter of Ecclesiastes, saying "Do not betray the king in your thought," which means that no subject ought to conspire against his lord.

It is also dangerous to complain about or disobey the laws of princes. In his twelfth chapter, Justin tells about Alexander, who became ruler of Persia due to the great victories that he had won. He wanted to be greeted according to the custom of the place, which was a kind of adoration, as we would call kneeling or speaking on one's knees, which was not the customary thing in Macedonia or other regions. But because there were complaints, Cantilenes the philosopher (who had been sent to him by Aristotle, because he could no longer abide the burden of traveling with him himself) harshly reproved Alexander, for which Alexander had him executed. And this means, says Valerius, that when Aristotle left Alexander, he left this Cantilenes in his place, for he was his disciple and was very wise. But Aristotle counselled his disciple not to speak of the vices of the prince behind his back for two reasons. First, it does not become a subject to shame his lord. Secondly, that as soon as these words have gone out of his mouth, they are reported to the king by flatterers. He advised him to speak little to Alexander, but when he did, that he ought speak cheerfully, so that his words could not put him in danger. Nor should he flatter him, but if cheerfully phrased, what he said would be acceptable. But this disciple did not follow his master's teaching, and he repented too late.

Another example from Valerius of not disobeying the laws of the prince, and concerning the philosopher that Alexander had killed because of contradicting his law, was the philosopher Demades* in Athens. When Alexander wanted to be adored as described above, he sent word to Athens and said that he wanted to be worshipped in this way. The Athenians, who were more accustomed than other people to respect ceremonies and laws, went to their council on this. It was the common opinion that they not do him an honor which was appropriate only for the gods. Then the wise man Demades, who knew well what could happen if they disobeyed the prince, said to them: "Be careful not to be so careful of the heavens that you lose the earth."

These things could be given as an example in any country, but merciful God has not put cruel and bloody princes against their people in France. Because of all the nations of the world, I dare say without flattery, it is true that are no more benign and humane princes than in France, and thus they ought all the more to be obeyed. And even if sometimes by chance it seems to the people that they are grieved and burdened, they should not believe that other places are less so, and even supposing that were true because of their chartered liberties that other peoples enjoy, yet they may have other services and usages that are more detrimental, like great wrongs done to them, or murders amongst themselves, because there is no justice which guards them or treats them in another way. And in spite of those who contradict me, I hold that of all the countries in Christendom, in this one the people commonly live better both because of the benevolence of princes without cruelty, and because of the courtesy and amiability of the people of this nation. And I do not say this out of favoritism, because I was not born here. But, God be my witness at the end, I say what I think! And since I have enquired about the government of other countries and I know there is no paradise on earth, I know that everywhere has its own troubles.

One could speak of these cruel princes of times past, and even in present times there would be enough to find. But because this could not be turned to good example, I will pass over them lightly. But on the subject of people burdened by the ruler, an amazingly false and dishonest trick was played on his people by the tyrant Denis.* This Denis was defeated in battle, so afterwards he went and plotted in great malice and evil, in order to recover his losses and expenses. He publicly announced to all his people and citizens, that he believed that the loss was due to sin since he had not fulfilled an old vow to the goddess Venus. If she would give him help and grace in battle so that he would be victorious, he vowed that on the feast day of the goddess and in her honor, all the ladies and young women of the country would give pleasure to any man that requested it. But because he had not fulfilled his vow after the victory in battle, Venus had avenged herself on him for having defrauded her. In this most recent battle, she had caused his defeat. And so to satisfy the goddess, on her solemn feast-day, he ordered all the ladies and young girls to dress themselves in their richest apparel and with all their jewels. And those who had no jewels of their own were to borrow some. Then they were to go to the temple and from there they would be brought to the public square. But every man should be made to swear not to touch them. Because of this oath, the foolish people of this land believed the king and consented that their wives and daughters be brought there because it seemed to them that this would appease and satisfy the goddess without threat to either the honor or the chastity of their wives and daughters. So all the women, dressed as well and as richly as they could, went to the temple. But Denis their king, had a different plan in mind. Having lied about this, he knew by their clothing and jewels the riches of his people and his burghers. So it seemed to him that he could burden them with greater taxes, and with that he sent some people to the temple to rob them of their rich robes and jewels and the richest matrons were forced by beatings and torture to reveal the savings of their husbands.

This Denis, who was king of Sicily, could well be called a bad prince. But so that no one has the desire to imitate him, it should be known that, as often happens, an evil life attracts an evil end, and his end was very bad. After he had done this evil deed, he was villainously slain by his own people. His son, who was also named Denis, succeeded him but also had a bad end: he was deposed as ruler and afterwards taught children at a school in Corinth to earn his living. Thus the child bears the burden of the misdeeds and evil of his father. As it is written in Holy Scripture, "the fathers eat sour grapes and their children suffer from toothache." It is also written, "our fathers sin and we bear their iniquities."

Still on the subject of bad princes, from which God guard us, there was once a king in Egypt named Ptholomeus Phiton, who among other vices was debauched and lecherous. And he was named Phiton, says Valerius, because Phiton is synonymous with increase and augmentation of vice, for because of his lechery, he committed many crimes and infinite evils, for which reason he died a villainous death and is defamed in memory.

# Chapter 8 On merchants

As we discussed before, the merchant class is very necessary, and without it neither the estate of kings and princes nor even the polities of cities and countries could exist. For by the industry of their labor, all kinds of people are provided for without their having to make everything themselves, because, if they have money, merchants bring from afar all things necessary and proper for human beings to live. For it is a good thing that persons can occupy different offices in the world. For otherwise, one would be so busy with trying to make a living that no one could attend to other aspects of knowledge – thus God and reason have provided well.

And for the good that they do for everyone, this class of people – loyal merchants who in buying and selling, in exchanging things one for another by taking money or by other honest means – are to be loved and commended as necessary, and in many countries are held in high esteem. And there is no important citizen in any city who is not involved with trade, however, they are not considered thereby less noble. So Venice, Genoa, and other places have the most rich and powerful merchants who seek out goods of all kinds, which they distribute all over the world. And thus is the world served all kinds of things, and without doubt, they act honestly. I hold that they have a meritorious office, accepted by God and permitted and approved by the laws.

These people ought to be well advised in their deeds, honest in their labor, truthful in their words, clever in what they do, because they have to know how to buy and resell things at such a price as not to lose money, and ought to be well informed about whether there are enough goods and where they are going short and when to buy and when to sell – otherwise their business will be gone.

They ought to be honest in their work, that is that they ought not, under threat of damnation and awful punishment of the body, treat their goods with any tricks to make them seem better than they are in order to deceive people so that they might be more expensive or more quickly sold, because every trade is punished when there is fraud in one. And those that practice deception ought not to be called merchants but rather deceivers and evil doers. Above all, merchants should be truthful in words and in promises, accustomed to speaking and keeping the truth so that a simple promise by a merchant will be believed as certain as by a contract. And those that keep their promises and are always found honest should prefer to suffer damage rather than fail to keep an agreement, which is a very good and honest custom, and it would please God, if others in France and elsewhere would do the same. Although there may be some that do wrong, I hold that by the mercy of God, there are those who are good, honest, and true. May God keep them rich, honorable and worthy of trust! For it is very good for a country and of great value to a prince and to the common polity when a city has trade and an abundance of merchants. This is why cities on the sea or major rivers are commonly rich and large, because of the goods that are brought by merchants from far away to be delivered there. So these people ought to be of fair and honest life without pomp or arrogance and ought to serve God in courage and reverence and to give alms generously from what

God has given them, as one finds among those who give a tenth of
their goods to the poor and who found many chapels, places of prayer,
and hospitals for the poor. And so there are those of such goodness
that if God pleases, they truly deserve merit in heaven and goodness
and honor in the world.

## Chapter 9 The third class of the people

Next comes the third rank of the people who are artisans and agricul-
tural workers, which we call the last part of the body politic and who
are like legs and feet, according to Plutarch, and who should be
exceptionally well watched over and cared for so that they suffer no
hurt, for that which hurts them can dangerously knock the whole
body down. It is therefore more necessary to take good care and
provide for them, since for the health of the body, they do not cease
to go "on foot." The varied jobs that the artisans do are necessary
for the human body and it cannot do without them, just as a human
body cannot go without its feet. It would shamefully and uselessly
drag itself in great pain on its hands and body without them, just as,
he says, if the republic excluded laborers and artisans, it could not
sustain itself. Thus although some think little of the office of the
craftsman that the clerics call "artisans," yet it is good, noble, and
necessary, as said before. And among all the other good things which
exist, so this one should be even more praised because, of all the
worldly estates, this one comes closest to science. Artisans put into
practice what science teaches, as Aristotle says in his *Metaphysics*,
because their works are the result of sciences, such as geometry,
which is the science of measurement and proportion without which
no craft could exist. To this a writer testifies, saying that the Athenians wanted to make a marvelous altar to Minerva, the goddess of
wisdom, and because they wanted a notable and beautiful work above
all, they sought advice from the best teachers. They went to the
philosopher Plato as the most accomplished master of all the sciences,
but he sent them to Euclid* instead as the master of the art of
measurement, because he created geometry which is read everyday
in general studies.

And from this can one see that artisans follow science. For masons,
carpenters, and all other workers in whatever crafts work according
to the teachings of the sciences. "To be praised is to master a craft,"

says Valerius, "so that art will follow nature." When a worker properly copies a thing which nature has made, as when a painter who is a great artist makes the portrait of a man so lifelike and so well, that everyone recognizes him, or when he makes a recognizable bird or other beast; so too the sculptor of images makes a likeness, and so on. And so some say that art is the "apess" or the "ape" of nature, because a monkey imitates many of the ways of a man, just as art imitates many of the works of nature.

But nonetheless, they say, art can not imitate everything, so one ought to praise the skillful in art and believe those who have experience in it, for there is no doubt that no one speaks as appropriately of a thing as the one who knows it. And I believe the most skilled artisans of all crafts are more commonly in Paris than elsewhere, which is an important and beautiful thing.

But to speak a little of the fact of their habits: I would to God they pleased God, but in themselves, for it would be pleasing to God if their lives were more sober and less licentious as is appropriate to their estate. For lechery in taverns and the luxuries they use in Paris can lead to many evil and unsuitable things. Aristotle speaks of the voluptuous life that such people and those like them lead, saying that many seem like beasts because they choose lechery before any other pleasures.

And on the false opinion that gluttons have: In the second chapter of Wisdom, Holy Scripture says that they believe "the time of our life is short and full of troubles and in the end we have no rest, and so we use our youth to follow our desires, and we fill ourselves with wine and meat, and in everything leave the traces of our joy." And without doubt, similar foolish and vain words can often be heard not only from simple people but from others believed wise for their position. So the people especially ought to heed preaching and sermons on the Word of God, since for the most part they are not educated in the teachings of Holy Scripture.

Good exhortations and sermons are beneficial for Christians to hear, as Justin recounts in the twentieth book of Trogus Pompeius about the city of Croton. They were pagans and unbelievers, and Pythagoras the philosopher, also a pagan, reformed them through his exhortations on their evil lives. For while the people there were corrupt and inclined to gluttony, vice, and lechery, they were brought to continence and a pure life by the intervention of Pythagoras. This philosopher castigated most the vice of lechery and showed that because of it many cities had gone to ruin. He taught ladies and men the doctrine of honesty and chastity, and to be sober in their food and drink. And so Pythagoras, by his wise admonitions, made the ladies put aside their fancy clothes and the men their gluttonous lives. And for the twenty years that he lived there he continued his instruction. Justin says that in the city of Methaponthus in Puilla, from which Pythagoras came, people had so great a reverence for the house in which he was born that they made it a temple and adored Pythagoras as God because of the good he had done.

Great is the need in many places for such a one, and also for people wanting to put to work that which he taught.

## Chapter 10 On simple laborers

On the subject of simple laborers of the earth, what should I say of them when so many people despise and oppress them? Of all the estates, they are the most necessary, those who are cultivators of the earth which feed and nourish the human creature, without whom the world would end in little time. And really those who do them so many evils do not take heed of what they do, for anyone who considers himself a rational creature will hold himself obligated to them. It is a sin to be ungrateful for as many services as they give us! And really it is very much the feet which support the body politic, for they support the body of every person with their labor. They do nothing that is unpraiseworthy. God has made their office acceptable, first, because the two heads of the world, from whom all human life is descended, were laborers of the earth. The first head was Adam, the first father, of whom it is written in the second chapter of Genesis, "God took the first man and put him in a paradise of pleasures, to work, cultivate and take care of it." And from this Scripture one can draw two arguments to prove the honesty of labor: The first is that God commanded it and made it first of all crafts. The second, that this craft was created during the state of innocence.

The second head of the world was Noah from whom, after the flood, all humans are descended. It is written in the ninth chapter that Noah was a laborer, and after the flood he put himself to work on the land and planted vineyards. And so our fathers, the ancient patriarchs were all cultivators of the earth and shepherds of beasts (whose stories I will not tell you for the sake of brevity), and in the olden days it was not an ignoble office nor unpraiseworthy.

In his *History of the Romans*, Florus* tells us how Diocletian, Emperor of Rome, after many battles and victories, went for the rest of his life to the village called Sallon and his occupation was working on the land. Long after, the rulers of Rome were lacking good government, so Lentulius and Galerius sent to this admirable man to ask that he return to Rome and take over the empire. "Ah," he said, "if you had seen the beautiful cabbages that I planted with my own hands, you would not require me to return to the empire." And this was to say that he had more peace of mind in his state of poverty than in carrying a burden so large and perilous as an empire.

And on this subject, in the third chapter of the fourth book Valerius tells of Actilus, the very worthy Roman who was taken from his work to be emperor. As he worked at his plough in the field, knights came to seek him, and he was made chief and leader of the whole Roman army. And he whose hands had been hardened by labor at the plow, after he had left the leadership of the army, reestablished the republic by his noble courage and with his hands. Said Valerius, "the hand which had governed a team of oxen behind the plow took up governing battle chariots." And after many noble and great victories, he was not ashamed to leave the dignity of emperor and return to the work he had left behind.

Because of these stories, we can understand that the estate of simple laborer or others of low rank should not be denigrated, as others would do. When those of the highest rank choose for their retirement a humble life of simplicity as the best for the soul and the body, then they are surely rich who voluntarily are poor. For they have no fear of being betrayed, poisoned, robbed, or envied, for their wealth is in sufficiency. For no one is rich without it, nor is there any other wealth.

To confirm this, I will tell what Valerius said about sufficiency and about a very rich man who was very poor in having it. There was, Valerius said, a King in Lydia, who was named Gyges.* His wealth was reputed to be so great that he went to ask the god Apollo whether there was anyone more happy than he. Apollo answered him that Agamis Soplidius was happier than he was. This Agamis was the poorest in Arcadia and he was very old. He never left his little field and was content with the small yield on which he lived and that which he had. Thus one can see how Apollo understood happiness to be sufficiency and not wealth, because in wealth one cannot have sufficiency, at least, not security, but instead a lot of concerns, and a plenitude of fears and worries. And so, King Gyges, who believed that the god ought to confirm that no one was happier than he, was mistaken in his vain opinion, and learned what pure and firm wealth and happiness were.

Anaxagoras* agreed that happiness is to have sufficiency. In the prologue to the Almagest, Ptolemy says "he is happy who does not care in whose hands the world is." And that this saying is true is proven by all the sages, the poets, and especially, those perfect ones who have chosen a pure and poor life for their greatest surety. For although one can be saved in any estate, nonetheless it is more difficult to pass by flames and not be burned. There is no doubt that the estate of the poor which everyone despises has many good and worthy persons in purity of life.

## Chapter 11 Christine concludes her book

I have come, God be praised, to the end I intended, that is I bring to an end the present book, which began, as Plutarch described, with the head of the body of the polity which is understood to be the princes. From them, I very humbly request first that the head of all, the King of France, and afterwards the princes and all those of their noble blood, that the diligent labor of writing by the humble creature Christine – this present work, as well as her others such as they might be – are agreeable to them. And since she is a woman of little knowledge, if by ignorance any faults are found, let her be pardoned and her good intention better known, for she intends only good to be the effect of her work. And I beg in payment from those living and their successors, the very noble kings and other French princes, in remembrance of my sayings in times to come when my soul is out of my body, that they would pray to God for me, requesting indulgence and remission of my sins.

And likewise, I ask of French knights, nobles, and generally of all, no matter from where they might be, that if they have any pleasure in the hours they saw or heard read from my little nothings, that they think of me and say an Our Father. And in the same way,

I wish the universal people – the three estates and the whole together – that God by His holy mercy desire to maintain and increase them from better to better in all perfection of souls and bodies. Amen.

Here it ends.

# Index

# Index

# Index

Pythagoras, xxxviii, 28, 100, 106, 107

rank, xxii, xxxviii, xli, 9, 10, 14, 17, 19,
  20, 24, 26, 27, 30, 38, 50, 51, 52,
  75, 99, 105, 108
republic, xxxiv, 22, 27, 35, 36, 41, 42,
  45, 63, 77, 92, 105, 108
*Rhetoric*, xxi, 36, 46, 48, 54
rights, 19
Roman, xvii, xviii, xix, xxii, xxxiii, xxxvi,
  xxxix, xli, 14, 21, 22, 25, 26, 28, 32,
  33, 35, 41, 48, 49, 61, 66, 67, 69,
  73, 74, 76, 78, 79, 84, 87, 108
Rome, xxi, xxiii, xxxiv, xl, 13–15,
  20–24, 26, 29, 33, 34, 40, 41, 45,
  48–52, 61–65, 68, 69, 72, 74,
  76–79, 84–86, 88, 98, 108
rule, xvii, xviii, xl, 12, 15, 25, 36, 38,
  46, 48, 50, 79, 92
rule of life, xxxix, 3, 4

Saint Augustine, xxxix
Saint Paul, xxxix, 93
Sallust, xxxix, 51, 91
Sappho, xxxix, 97
science, xxxiii, xxxiv, 40, 41, 39, 43–46,
  69, 70, 105
Scipio Africanus Major, xxxiii, xxxix,
  21, 25, 50, 55, 62, 70, 82
Scipio Africanus Minor, xl, 79–80, 88
Senate, xl, 14, 36, 49, 51, 72, 76–78
Seneca, xix, xxi, xxxvii, xl, 17, 27, 53,
  96, 98, 100
Sertorius, xl, 71, 88
servitude, xl, 20, 68
sheep, xl, 16, 17, 19
simple, xxi, xxxix, 5, 25, 54, 58, 100,
  104, 106–108
sin, 13, 14, 43, 102, 103, 107
Socrates, xxxiii, 56, 96, 98, 100
Solinus, xxxix, 69

Solon, xxxiii, xxxviii, xl, 34, 37, 46
soul, xix, xxii, 12, 15, 24, 26, 35, 37,
  43, 48, 57, 65, 98, 108, 109
sovereign, xl, 4, 15, 22, 30, 56, 71
student, students, xxii, xxiii, 41, 63,
  95–97, 98

Tarquin, xli, 85
Thales, xli, 44
Themistocles, xli, 56, 77
Tiberias, xli, 19
Tigranes, xli, 29, 30, 63
Titus, xxxiv, xli, 27, 52, 69, 72, 77, 84,
  86, 93
triumph, xviii, 22, 51, 63, 69, 77
Trogus Pompeius, xli, 94, 106
Tully, see Cicero

Valerius, xxi–xxii, xli, 4, 9, 13–15,
  19–26, 31–34, 36, 38–41, 45, 46,
  49–55, 57, 59–61, 64–69, 71, 72,
  76, 77, 79, 82–84, 86, 88, 94,
  96–98, 100, 101, 103, 106, 108
Varro, xli, 69
Vegetius, xxii, xli, 49, 60, 70, 71
Vesta, xli, 13
vice, vices, xx, 3, 5, 13, 14, 17, 27, 43,
  46, 49, 53, 54, 55, 75, 78, 80, 81,
  83, 96, 101, 103, 106, 107
virtue, xviii, xxi, xxii, 3–5, 7–9, 11, 12,
  15, 21–28, 30, 35, 36, 37, 38, 43,
  44, 46, 49, 51, 53–58, 60–63, 65,
  75, 78, 79, 81, 91, 93, 96–98, 100
virtues, xviii, xx, xxii, 5, 7, 10, 11, 17,
  22, 26, 28, 31, 33, 37, 38, 41, 46,
  48, 55–59, 62, 75, 78

wisdom, xviii, xix, xx, xxiv, 13, 21, 22,
  24, 35–37, 39, 42, 47, 50, 71, 73,
  79, 82, 95–98, 100, 105

Xerxes, xli, 97

113

# Cambridge Texts in the History of Political Thought

*Titles published in the series thus far*

Aristotle *The Politics* and *The Constitution of Athens* (edited by Stephen Everson)
   0 521 48400 6 paperback
Arnold *Culture and Anarchy and other writings* (edited by Stefan Collini)
   0 521 37796 x paperback
Astell *Political Writings* (edited by Patricia Springborg)
   0 521 42845 9 paperback
Augustine *The City of God against the Pagans* (edited by R. W. Dyson)
   0 521 46843 4 paperback
Austin *The Province of Jurisprudence Determined* (edited by Wilfrid E. Rumble)
   0 521 44756 9 paperback
Bacon *The History of the Reign of King Henry VII* (edited by Brian Vickers)
   0 521 58663 1 paperback
Bakunin *Statism and Anarchy* (edited by Marshall Shatz)
   0 521 36973 8 paperback
Baxter *Holy Commonwealth* (edited by William Lamont)
   0 521 40580 7 paperback
Bayle *Political Writings* (edited by Sally L. Jenkinson)
   0 521 47677 1 paperback
Beccaria *On Crimes and Punishments and other writings* (edited by Richard Bellamy)
   0 521 47982 7 paperback
Bentham *Fragment on Government* (introduction by Ross Harrison)
   0 521 35929 5 paperback
Bernstein *The Preconditions of Socialism* (edited by Henry Tudor)
   0 521 39808 8 paperback
Bodin *On Sovereignty* (edited by Julian H. Franklin)
   0 521 34992 3 paperback
Bolingbroke *Political Writings* (edited by David Armitage)
   0 521 58697 6 paperback
Bossuet *Politics Drawn from the Very Words of Holy Scripture* (edited by Patrick Riley)
   0 521 36807 3 paperback
*The British Idealists* (edited by David Boucher)
   0 521 45951 6 paperback
Burke *Pre-Revolutionary Writings* (edited by Ian Harris)
   0 521 36800 6 paperback
Christine De Pizan *The Book of the Body Politic* (edited by Kate Langdon Forhan)
   0 521 42259 0 paperback
Cicero *On Duties* (edited by M. T. Griffin and E. M. Atkins)
   0 521 34835 8 paperback
Cicero *On the Commonwealth and On the Laws* (edited by James E. G. Zetzel)
   0 521 45959 1 paperback

Comte *Early Political Writings* (edited by H. S. Jones)
  0 521 46923 6 paperback
*Conciliarism and Papalism* (edited by J. H. Burns and Thomas M. Izbicki)
  0 521 47674 7 paperback
Constant *Political Writings* (edited by Biancamaria Fontana)
  0 521 31632 4 paperback
Dante *Monarchy* (edited by Prue Shaw)
  0 521 56781 5 paperback
Diderot *Political Writings* (edited by John Hope Mason and Robert Wokler)
  0 521 36911 8 paperback
*The Dutch Revolt* (edited by Martin van Gelderen)
  0 521 39809 6 paperback
*Early Greek Political Thought from Homer to the Sophists* (edited by Michael Gagarin
  and Paul Woodruff)
  0 521 43768 7 paperback
*The Early Political Writings of the German Romantics* (edited by
  Frederick C. Beiser)
  0 521 44951 0 paperback
*The English Levellers* (edited by Andrew Sharp)
  0 521 62511 4 paperback
Erasmus *The Education of a Christian Prince* (edited by Lisa Jardine)
  0 521 58811 1 paperback
Fenelon *Telemachus* (edited by Patrick Riley)
  0 521 45662 2 paperback
Ferguson *An Essay on the History of Civil Society* (edited by Fania Oz-Salzberger)
  0 521 44736 4 paperback
Filmer *Patriarcha and Other Writings* (edited by Johann P. Sommerville)
  0 521 39903 3 paperback
Fletcher *Political Works* (edited by John Robertson)
  0 521 43994 9 paperback
Sir John Fortescue *On the Laws and Governance of England* (edited by
  Shelley Lockwood)
  0 521 58996 7 paperback
Fourier *The Theory of the Four Movements* (edited by Gareth Stedman Jones and Ian
  Patterson)
  0 521 35693 8 paperback
Gramsci *Pre-Prison Writings* (edited by Richard Bellamy)
  0 521 42307 4 paperback
Guicciardini *Dialogue on the Government of Florence* (edited by Alison Brown)
  0 521 45623 1 paperback
Harrington *A Commonwealth of Oceana* and *A System of Politics* (edited by
  J. G. A. Pocock)
  0 521 42329 5 paperback

Hegel *Elements of the Philosophy of Right* (edited by Allen W. Wood and
H. B. Nisbet)
0 521 34888 9 paperback
Hegel *Political Writings* (edited by Laurence Dickey and H. B. Nisbet)
0 521 45979 3 paperback
Hobbes *On the Citizen* (edited by Michael Silverthorne and Richard Tuck)
0 521 43780 6 paperback
Hobbes *Leviathan* (edited by Richard Tuck)
0 521 56797 1 paperback
Hobhouse *Liberalism and Other Writings* (edited by James Meadowcroft)
0 521 43726 1 paperback
Hooker *Of the Laws of Ecclesiastical Polity* (edited by A. S. McGrade)
0 521 37908 3 paperback
Hume *Political Essays* (edited by Knud Haakonssen)
0 521 46639 3 paperback
King James VI and I *Political Writings* (edited by Johann P. Sommerville)
0 521 44729 1 paperback
Jefferson *Political Writings* (edited by Joyce Appleby and Terence Ball)
0 521 64841 6 paperback
John of Salisbury *Policraticus* (edited by Cary Nederman)
0 521 36701 8 paperback
Kant *Political Writings* (edited by H. S. Reiss and H. B. Nisbet)
0 521 39837 1 paperback
Knox *On Rebellion* (edited by Roger A. Mason)
0 521 39988 2 paperback
Kropotkin *The Conquest of Bread and other writings* (edited by Marshall Shatz)
0 521 45990 7 paperback
Lawson *Politica sacra et civilis* (edited by Conal Condren)
0 521 39248 9 paperback
Leibniz *Political Writings* (edited by Patrick Riley)
0 521 35899 X paperback
*The Levellers* (edited by Andrew Sharp)
0 521 62511 4 paperback
Locke *Political Essays* (edited by Mark Goldie)
0 521 47861 8 paperback
Locke *Two Treatises of Government* (edited by Peter Laslett)
0 521 35730 6 paperback
Loyseau *A Treatise of Orders and Plain Dignities* (edited by Howell A. Lloyd)
0 521 45624 X paperback
*Luther and Calvin on Secular Authority* (edited by Harro Höpfl)
0 521 34986 9 paperback
Machiavelli *The Prince* (edited by Quentin Skinner and Russell Price)
0 521 34993 1 paperback

de Maistre *Considerations on France* (edited by Isaiah Berlin and Richard Lebrun)
  0 521 46628 8 paperback
Malthus *An Essay on the Principle of Population* (edited by Donald Winch)
  0 521 42972 2 paperback
Marsiglio of Padua *Defensor minor* and *De translatione Imperii* (edited by
  Cary Nederman)
  0 521 40846 6 paperback
Marx *Early Political Writings* (edited by Joseph O'Malley)
  0 521 34994 X paperback
Marx *Later Political Writings* (edited by Terrell Carver)
  0 521 36739 5 paperback
James Mill *Political Writings* (edited by Terence Ball)
  0 521 38748 5 paperback
J. S. Mill *On Liberty*, with *The Subjection of Women* and *Chapters on Socialism* (edited
  by Stefan Collini)
  0 521 37917 2 paperback
Milton *Political Writings* (edited by Martin Dzelzainis)
  0 521 34866 8 paperback
Montesquieu *The Spirit of the Laws* (edited by Anne M. Cohler, Basia Carolyn Miller
  and Harold Samuel Stone)
  0 521 36974 6 paperback
More *Utopia* (edited by George M. Logan and Robert M. Adams)
  0 521 40318 9 paperback
Morris *News from Nowhere* (edited by Krishan Kumar)
  0 521 42233 7 paperback
Nicholas of Cusa *The Catholic Concordance* (edited by Paul E. Sigmund)
  0 521 56773 4 paperback
Nietzsche *On the Genealogy of Morality* (edited by Keith Ansell-Pearson)
  0 521 40610 2 paperback
Paine *Political Writings* (edited by Bruce Kuklick)
  0 521 36678 X paperback
Plato *Statesman* (edited by Julia Annas and Robin Waterfield)
  0 521 44778 X paperback
Price *Political Writings* (edited by D. O. Thomas)
  0 521 40969 1 paperback
Priestley *Political Writings* (edited by Peter Miller)
  0 521 42561 1 paperback
Proudhon *What is Property?* (edited by Donald R. Kelley and
  Bonnie G. Smith)
  0 521 40556 4 paperback
Pufendorf *On the Duty of Man and Citizen according to Natural Law* (edited by James
  Tully)
  0 521 35980 5 paperback

*The Radical Reformation* (edited by Michael G. Baylor)
0 521 37948 2 paperback
Rousseau *The Discourses and other early political writings* (edited by
Victor Gourevitch)
0 521 42445 3 paperback
Rousseau *The Social Contract and other later political writings* (edited by
Victor Gourevitch)
0 521 42446 1 paperback
Seneca *Moral and Political Essays* (edited by John Cooper and John Procope)
0 521 34818 8 paperback
Sidney *Court Maxims* (edited by Hans W. Blom, Eco Haitsma Mulier and
Ronald Janse)
0 521 46736 5 paperback
Sorel *Reflections on Violence* (edited by Jeremy Jennings)
0 521 55910 3 paperback
Spencer *The Man versus the State* and *The Proper Sphere of Government*
(edited by John Offer)
0 521 43740 7 paperback
Stirner *The Ego and Its Own* (edited by David Leopold)
0 521 45647 9 paperback
Thoreau *Political Writings* (edited by Nancy Rosenblum)
0 521 47675 5 paperback
*Utopias of the British Enlightenment* (edited by Gregory Claeys)
0 521 45590 1 paperback
Vitoria *Political Writings* (edited by Anthony Pagden and Jeremy Lawrance)
0 521 36714 X paperback
Voltaire *Political Writings* (edited by David Williams)
0 521 43727 X paperback
Weber *Political Writings* (edited by Peter Lassman and Ronald Speirs)
0 521 39719 7 paperback
William of Ockham *A Short Discourse on Tyrannical Government* (edited by
A. S. McGrade and John Kilcullen)
0 521 35803 5 paperback
William of Ockham *A Letter to the Friars Minor and other writings* (edited by
A. S. McGrade and John Kilcullen)
0 521 35804 3 paperback
Wollstonecraft *A Vindication of the Rights of Men* and *A Vindication of the Rights of
Woman* (edited by Sylvana Tomaselli)
0 521 43633 8 paperback

CPSIA information can be obtained
at www.ICGtesting.com
Printed in the USA
LVHW030116030821
694324LV00005B/928